LIFE
EVERLASTING

Jesus, I Trust in You

The original image of St. Faustina's vision of the Divine Mercy
of Jesus, painted by Eugeniusz Kazimirowski in 1934.

LIFE EVERLASTING

Catholic Devotions and Mysteries for the Everyday Seeker

GARY JANSEN

A TarcherPerigee Book

tarcherperigee

An imprint of Penguin Random House LLC
375 Hudson Street
New York, New York 10014

Permissions appear on page 291.

TarcherPerigee with tp colophon is a registered trademark
of Penguin Random House LLC.

Most TarcherPerigee books are available at special quantity discounts for
bulk purchase for sales promotions, premiums, fund-raising, and educational needs.
Special books or book excerpts also can be created to fit specific needs.
For details, write: SpecialMarkets@penguinrandomhouse.com.

Library of Congress Cataloging-in-Publication Data

Names: Jansen, Gary, author.
Title: Life everlasting : Catholic devotions and mysteries for the everyday
seeker / by Gary Jansen.
Description: New York : TarcherPerigee, 2018.
Identifiers: LCCN 2017036127 (print) | LCCN 2018001611 (ebook) | ISBN
9780525503866 (ebook) | ISBN 9780399162220 (pbk.)
Subjects: LCSH: Spiritual life—Catholic Church. | Catholic Church—Prayers
and devotions.
Classification: LCC BX2350.3 (ebook) | LCC BX2350.3 .J364 2018 (print) | DDC
248.4/82—dc23
LC record available at https://lccn.loc.gov/2017036127

Printed in the United States of America
3   5   7   9   10   8   6   4   2

Book design by Elke Sigal

For

Roseanne Jansen
Frances Poppi
Maura Zagrans
Kathryn Lopez

CONTENTS

Part I ⦙ The Awakening

Part II ⦙ The Path

Part III ⦙ The Devotions

CONTENTS

Part I

The Awakening

He said to his disciples, "Therefore I tell you, do not worry about your life, what you will eat, or about your body, what you will wear. For life is more than food, and the body more than clothing. Consider the ravens: they neither sow nor reap, they have neither storehouse nor barn, and yet God feeds them. Of how much more value are you than the birds! And can any of you by worrying add a single hour to your span of life? If then you are not able to do so small a thing as that, why do you worry about the rest? Consider the lilies, how they grow: they neither toil nor spin; yet I tell you, even Solomon in all his glory was not clothed like one of these. But if God so clothes the grass of the field, which is alive today and tomorrow is thrown into the oven, how much more will he clothe you—you of little faith! And do not keep striving for what you are to eat and what you are to drink, and do not keep worrying. For it is the nations of the world that strive after all these things, and your Father knows that you need them. Instead, strive for his kingdom, and these things will be given to you as well.

—LUKE 12:22–31

For the mystery of life can only be known by being lived.

—THOMAS MERTON, *THE LIVING BREAD*

Don't fear failure, man. Fear mediocrity.

—SOMEBODY WHO LOOKED LIKE JESUS ON THE SUBWAY

CHAPTER 1

How Big Is Your God?

I see something of God each hour of the twenty-four, and
each moment then,
In the faces of men and women I see God, and in my own
face in the glass;
I find letters from God dropped in the street, and every one
is signed by God's name,
And I leave them where they are, for I know that where-
soe'er I go,
Others will punctually come forever and ever.

—WALT WHITMAN

Your life depends upon this book.

The pages that follow are a spiritual first aid kit for those moments in our lives when we scrape our souls against the jagged surfaces of everyday life. Feeling unfulfilled in your job? Confused in a relationship? Short on money? Suffering from an illness? Trying to sell your house quickly? Or do you just feel lost in your own thoughts and emotions and as though you have tried everything possible to break free from being overwhelmed? If you've answered yes to any of these, well, there's just one thing to do: Drop to your knees and pray. But don't do it alone. Ask Jesus, the Virgin Mary, the saints, and the angels to be by your side.

This book is about Catholic devotions—prayers, meditations, and small actions you can take right now that will assist you in directing your life toward the greater good, helping you to find solace, healing, and direction when all seems lost. Think of them as a form of crisis intervention or spiritual 911—methods of communication that not only bring us closer to God but also offer reassurances that we are never, ever alone.

Though there are many ways of praying, devotions often involve some form of intercessory prayer, or praying on behalf of another. When we pray to saints, angels, or the Virgin Mary, we are asking them for help—assurance that we're not alone and assistance in helping us to know God better. Moreover, we are asking them to pray for us, just the way you may ask me to pray for you during a difficult time. Not many people would object to a prayer on their behalf, would they? But there is a big difference between me praying for you, and our friends in heaven praying for you. As much as I *want* to be super close to God, the saints, angels, and Mary *are* in union with him. So they have more knowledge, compassion, and influence in the heavenly realm than you and I. We reach out to these heavenly helpers not as if they were gods, but as if they were friends with solid advice or experts who can shed light on a problem.

This may all sound like some obscure practice, but consider this: A seventeenth-century cartographer gave Cupertino, California, the home of Apple, its name after his prayers and devotions to the levitating mystic St. Joseph Cupertino helped him find his way through the wild country of what is now the Santa

Cruz mountain range. Musician Jack White's mother named him after St. John the Baptist. Pope John Paul II had a lifelong dedication to the Virgin Mary and cites her intercession as what saved his life during an assassination attempt in 1981 (is it a coincidence that the attempt took place on the feast day of the apparition of the Virgin Mary known as Our Lady of Fatima?). Actor Danny Thomas's devotion to St. Jude led to the founding of the St. Jude's Children's Research Hospital, an organization that provides free medical care to children with cancer. Acclaimed author Paulo Coelho, the international bestselling author of *The Alchemist*, eventually developed an affection for the Immaculate Conception (another name for Jesus's mother) when he returned to his Catholic faith after spending a number of his early years dabbling with drugs and black magic. Martin Sheen prays the Rosary. Comedian Jim Gaffigan and entertainer and actor Harry Connick Jr. both have a special devotion to the Divine Mercy of Jesus. Late-night TV host Stephen Colbert's favorite saint is Peter, Jesus's flawed friend who, regardless of all his thickheadedness, became the first pope. Actor and activist Gary Sinise finds comfort and meaning in Father Mychal Judge's "Lord, take me where you want me to go" prayer. Many call Father Judge, a chaplain for the New York City Fire Department, the Saint of 9/11; he died of blunt-force trauma to the head while serving the dead and injured in the North Tower of the World Trade Center. Hollywood producer Roma Downey upholds a devotion to the holy angels. Novelist Nicholas Sparks looks to St. Anthony to help him when he's absentminded. This is not to mention the millions of people around the world who turn to prayer and devotions when they are looking for miracles in their lives. And if you think nothing miraculous happens in our day and age, well, you might just be surprised . . .

Consider, for instance, Dafne Gutierrez, a mother in Phoenix who suffered from benign intracranial hypertension, which caused her to lose her sight in both eyes. In January 2016, Dafne began praying to St. Charbel Makhlouf, a nineteenth-century Lebanese monk, and visited his relics that were on display in a local church. After a blessing by a priest, the woman went home and felt that something inside her had changed. A week later her eyesight was restored to 20/20. As of now there is no medical explanation for her recovery.

Or consider the famous case of Monica Besra, from West Bengal, India. The woman suffered from a dangerous abdominal tumor that protruded from her body. Doctors were convinced she was going to die. The Missionaries of Charity, a religious congregation started by Mother Teresa in 1950, began taking care of the woman in May 1998. Over the next few months and after numerous treatments at local hospitals, Monica continued to deteriorate. In time, the pain became so intolerable Monica found it nearly impossible to sleep. The Catholic nuns in charge of her began praying to Mother Teresa (who had died a year earlier, in 1997). Asking their beloved founder to intercede with God for this woman, the sisters placed a devotional item, the Miraculous Medal of the Virgin Mary, on her stomach. Monica fell asleep. Hours later when she awoke, her engorged abdomen had flattened. She was no longer in pain. Medical professionals later confirmed that her tumor had vanished.

Then there is the report of Father Peter Smith, a priest in Glasgow, Scotland, who was suffering from cancer. According to the *Catholic News Agency* in February 2017, doctors "discovered a blood clot on [the priest's] lung and a deadly infection attacking body tissue from his hips to shoulders." Smith was not expected to live longer than forty-eight hours. But after he said prayers of intercession to Margaret Sinclair, a young Edinburgh nun who died in 1925 (and whom many believe should be declared a saint), the priest survived. As Father Smith explains, "We don't expect miracles—and I'm not sure I expected one either; after all, my cancer hasn't gone away—but I've been around long enough in ministry not to be surprised. I've seen it happen." By "it," Smith means the sometimes miraculous answer to prayers.

These three accounts are extraordinary and, some might say, sensationalistic. Critics will argue that any healings that took place were the result of previous medical treatments or the body's natural ability to repair itself. Moreover, there are plenty of people who have prayed and never seemed to experience miraculous effects this dramatically. But Father Smith is touching on something important here. Most of us don't expect miracles. Many think of them as parts of fairy tales, bits of wishful thinking, sometimes even a form of abuse that raises false hope for hopeless cases.

But what if expectation is a necessary component for allowing miracles into our lives? What if we need to think bigger? Father Smith experienced something extraordinary, though, as he admits, he may not have been focused on anything miraculous. Yet, he still prayed, which meant he was open to the mysterious healing power of prayer. It's hard to believe the priest wasn't hoping for a healing in the back of his mind.

What if we all expect too little from God? What if the God most of us believe in is too small? What if we embraced what Jesus, the archetypal miracle worker said: "Very truly, I tell you, the one who believes in me will also do the works that I do and, in fact, will do greater works than these. . . . If in my name you ask me for anything, I will do it" (John 14:12, 14)? What would happen if we *really* lived by these words? What would our lives be like? What would our world be like?

It would be heaven on earth.

Prayer and devotions draw us closer to Jesus, closer to God, and closer to heaven, and as we inch toward the eternal, we not only experience less worry and more peace, we become conduits for the miraculous. I know that for myself, prayer, devotions, and a healthy belief in miracles (meaning I believe God answers our prayers, but I'm not going to try and walk on water) have strengthened all aspects of my life—physical, emotional, and psychological. This mind-set moves us toward spiritual transformation, ways of bringing the marvels of healing, peace, compassion, mercy, and love to ourselves and the world around us.

As many Catholics know, devotions are the short practices found on the back of prayer cards, or they involve rosary beads or using small medals that can be found in churches or local religious bookstores. For those who may be new to devotions, these are time-honored spiritual traditions, many of which have survived for well over a thousand years because, well, they work.

The contents found in *Life Everlasting*—if followed and embraced with a healthy mix of desire, commitment, and faith—can radically alter your life for the better, ushering in a new awakening and a heightened awareness of God's abundance in your day-to-day life. Lost causes can be won by beseeching St. Jude, healings can occur by praying with the Miraculous Medal, prayers to St. Matthew (a tax collector and apostle of Jesus) can aid you during financial difficulties, and prayers to St. Gerard have been known to help mothers during difficult pregnancies. Though only God can work miracles, the practices in this book can help us live in a state of the miraculous by making us aware of the signs and moments when heaven and earth intersect in unsuspected and meaningful ways. And all it takes is the decision to do one simple thing: embrace a devotion with enthusiasm and faith.

Many people claim to be on a spiritual path. We pray, meditate, maybe go to church or synagogue, or practice yoga during our lunch hour. We may read some of the thousands of self-help or spirituality books that have been published over the past fifty years. We're trying. We're striving to answer the ineffable call that many of us feel inside for something else, something we don't understand, but something that makes us ask, "Is this it? Is this all there is? Or is there a secret meaning to our lives?" Yet, this holy longing, this yearning that sometimes grips our hearts and begs us to find something deeper and more meaningful, can often leave us feeling confused, empty, and lost.

Moreover, we live, like many generations before us, in a time of great anxiety. Our problems and challenges, of course, feel more pertinent because we're living through them right now. Terrorism, political divisions, economic uncertainty, cultural upheavals, shifting religious demographics, and the disturbing rise of drug abuse and addiction across the country leave many of us feeling confused, nervous, and irritable. In a pervasively digitally connected world, young people are prone to suffer from constant nervousness (and not just young people—more and more men and women ages thirty-five to fifty-four find themselves using social media more than ever before). We are in the midst of what author George Packer calls an unwinding, in which "everything changes and nothing lasts." Many of us want to take action—to do something—but we can't seem to move. We're standing in a road, there is a tractor trailer barreling down upon us, and all we can do is watch.

Yet, in many instances, we can move out of the way; all it takes is one small shift in a new direction to avoid disaster. Devotions can often be that simple shift.

Imagine for a moment what it would feel like to live a *mostly* worry-free life (let's not overpromise), a life in which you weren't afraid to be yourself, weren't afraid of not having enough money, weren't afraid that people would abandon you, weren't afraid of being on your own. A life in which you felt protected at all times. What would *your* life be like if you weren't anxious or uneasy?

In the past twenty years of my own spiritual journey I've come to realize that the times I felt close to God were the times I felt less tense in my life and most joyful. There is a direct correlation. When I prayed, things seemed to, well, open up. Questions were answered. Signposts appeared that pointed me in the right direction. And doors appeared that often led to new opportunities or fresh ways of thinking. I don't mean to say that help arrived in an instant, though there were plenty of times when this did happen. I share some of those stories in this book. And I don't mean to say that problems necessarily went away. But I certainly could deal with them better when I knew God was there to help me through life's ups and downs. Think about it: don't we often feel better if we call on a trusted friend or parent who reassures us that no matter what we're going through, he or she is there to support us? I know it works for me.

During my journey, I've also come to see the need for all of us to draw nearer to the sacred. The closer we draw to the light of God, the more radiant we become. There are many ways to do this, but what I've found to be most effective is to find something or someone you can dedicate your life to and then allow the transcendent to reveal itself to you.

All the great saints did this. St. Francis's dedication to the poor and to nature drew him closer to God. St. Thomas Aquinas experienced revelations of the Almighty through his commitment to expanding the intellect. St. Thérèse of Lisieux embraced God through the simple things in life, such as the beauty of flowers and the sound of her broom when she swept a floor. St. Catherine Labouré encountered God through her devotion to the Virgin Mary. St. John Bosco's pledge to help and educate children provided a unique doorway to the divine.

How does this relate to our lives of going to work, caring for a family, or trying to do some good in the world? Simply, the closer these saints got to God, the less they freaked out about the pains and challenges of everyday life. Why? They knew God had their backs. They knew they were protected. They knew that the Divine was always there to help them. As Italian mystic and saint Padre Pio once wrote, "I have so much confidence in Jesus that even if I saw hell opened up before me and found myself on the threshold of the abyss, I would not worry, I would not despair. I would trust him." Really consider those words for a moment. Imagine feeling so confident in life that you could be alone on the highest precipice, peering down into certain death, and not be afraid.

We too can experience a similar relationship with God—not to become saints, necessarily (who wants that pressure?), but to live in a perpetual state of reassurance, a guarantee that while all might seem dim in the visible world, there is a force in the invisible world that shines on us and can give us strength to endure anything. There are numerous ways to develop this relationship with God and to begin to experience this type of life. As Jesus says, "In my Father's house there are many dwelling places" (John 14:2), meaning there are various ways to sit in the presence of God. But one way that has proven to be fruitful for so many is through the devotions that are such an important part of the spiritual practice of the Catholic life. Though their names may sound unfamiliar to some, from the Most Holy Name to the Prayer of St. Michael, from the Rosary to the Stations of the Cross, from the Novena of the Sacred Heart to the Chaplet of the Divine Mercy, these simple acts of piety can help us connect with the ultimate spiritual power that not only protects us but also heals and inspires. And these practices aren't just for Catholics. For centuries, people, rich and poor, Jew and agnostic, have embraced many of these acts of piety. Thousands of Alcoholics Anonymous members, regardless of their background, often recite the Lord's Prayer and the Serenity Prayer before meetings. Protestants have been known to pray the Rosary as a way of developing their knowledge of the Bible. Evangelical pastor Rick Warren prays the Chaplet of the Divine Mercy. And after writer Franz Viktor Werfel, an Austrian Jew, narrowly escaped the Nazis in 1939, finding shelter and solace in a Catholic shrine in Lourdes, France, he kept a lifelong devotion to the Virgin Mary. Though he never converted to Catholicism, the kindness and charity he experienced during that tumultuous time led him to write the novel *The Song of Bernadette*, the true-life story of a young girl named Bernadette Soubirous (later St. Bernadette), who had visions of Jesus's mother in a cave in 1858 and discovered the miraculous waters of a new spring that healed many after the apparitions. The book spent more than a year on the *New York Times* bestseller list, later becoming a motion picture and winning four Oscars at the 1944 Academy Awards, and inspired millions around the world during the dark days of World War II.

Life Everlasting will help you to receive and experience the miraculous by introducing you to the sacred mysteries of Jesus, the saints, the Virgin Mary, and the angels. It will broaden your awareness of the power of faith and help keep your spiritual life in balance with all the demands of your busy day-to-day life. These are simple prayers and easy disciplines that can help you feel more fulfilled in your role as husband or wife, parent, family member, friend, breadwinner, parishioner, colleague, or even stranger to all the people you meet throughout the year.

It is important to note that this isn't a self-help book, but a God-help book. Most self-help books just don't work. Why? They rely on you—the self—to help yourself get through difficult times. As Einstein says, "We can't solve problems by using the same kind of thinking we used when we created them." Instead, we need to turn to a higher power, a higher level of consciousness; we need to turn to God and his emissaries, the saints and the angels, who are there to help us in our times of need and guide us toward nourishment and wholeness.

HOW THIS BOOK WORKS

This book is meant to serve as a prologue to the spiritual life. As your tour guide, so to speak, I offer you three options for using the chapters that follow (but by all means, feel free to wander about on your own).

First, for those looking for more information on prayer and devotions in general, ideas on how we can engage not only our minds but also our hearts in prayer, and guidance for how to pray effectively, then just stay with me and keep on reading. Part I offers some further thoughts on the importance of prayer in our daily lives. Part II proposes seven steps to keep in mind on your prayer journey.

Second, for those of you who are eager to get to the devotional practices, please skip ahead to Part III. This section serves as a prayer book and offers a number of traditional devotions on the saints, angels, Mary, and Jesus as well as some practical ideas, exercises, and personal stories about how these practices affected my life (and hopefully will affect yours too).

Third, if this is an emergency and you need a lifeline thrown immediately, the appendix "Spiritual 911" offers a number of prayers you can use when your life is in crisis. The devotional life is about developing a steady relationship with God through your everyday life. But every once in a while you might find yourself in a precarious position and in need of serious refocusing. These prayers can help if you're suffering through a divorce, if you've been diagnosed with an illness, if you're experiencing a bout of depression, or if you've simply lost your keys and need to get the kids to school on time.

Though this book offers a wide range of devotions, this is by no means meant to be an exhaustive work. My selections here account for but a fraction of the prayers that are practiced by people around the world every day. I have made these particular suggestions in order to appeal to a wide readership of Catholic as well as non-Catholic readers (though, don't get me wrong, these are all pretty Catholic practices). My hope is not so much to preach to the choir as it is to invite you to hang with me and talk about God.

Moreover, of all the books I've written, this is one of my most personal. I will draw on my own private and intimate experiences with various devotions and share with you how these prayers affected me, changed my life, and helped me feel safe during challenging times. My hope is that your encounters with these sacred acts of piety might affect you in similarly rewarding ways.

Please do not think that the goal is to pray *all* of the devotions every day. Think of this book as a field guide to some time-honored traditions. Even so, you should try to pray every day, or as often as you can. As you read, find a prayer or practice that resonates with you. Maybe you want to get to know the angels better in hopes of getting to know Jesus better. Then make that practice a daily ritual. You don't have to tell anyone about your new practice unless you want to share it with someone you trust. Devotions are by their very nature personal acts. This is meant not to promote secrecy but to make the time you spend with God special and personal.

The practice of prayer is the practice of cultivating a good habit, which means it can take some time to develop. We need to be patient with ourselves. If you've never prayed for extended periods of time, it's a lot like if you've never run long distances. Most people realize they need to build up to a marathon, which means maybe they run a lap a day for a week before they try to run a mile, and then they run a couple of miles before they try for a 5K. The same applies to prayer. We should take it slow at first so as not to become overwhelmed and frustrated. In our technological age in which most people in the west own a cell phone, life can sometimes get away from us. I've found it helpful to set an alarm every day to remind me to take a few minutes to pray. You can do this in the morning, right before lunch, or anytime during the day. I set mine for three p.m.; it has been known to go off during work meetings. A quick press of a button silences the alarm, but at that moment, even if only briefly, my attention is centered on God.

And just as in physical fitness our bodies can become accustomed to a certain exercise and we plateau as a result, so too may we plateau in prayer. This does not mean that we, say, stop doing the bench press exercise if that's the one we always gravitate to when we're in the gym. No, the bench press is one of the foundations of muscle development—but it is by no means the only exercise we need to do in order to be physically fit. What we do is add other exercises that stimulate other muscles. In this way, the devotions in this book are meant to stimulate different parts of your soul. Just as a diamond is multifaceted and demonstrates its radiance in different ways depending on how you hold it up to the light, these acts are many sided and capable of revealing the multifaceted nature of God, Jesus, Mary, the saints, and the angels.

Before we move on, I'd like to tell you a little about my journey to devotion.

I was for most of my life a professional worrywart. And I was good at it. From the moment I woke up in the morning, I'd waste no time running through an assortment of mental movies in my head—high-budget disaster films, like those that often star Dwayne "The Rock" Johnson. Only mine weren't about giant earthquakes or tsunamis (okay, maybe sometimes they were). No. My films were about whether I might fail a test; would I be promoted at my job; would my train be late yet again; was that mole on my hand cancerous. I worried about ozone layers, the crime rate, carbon emissions, the size or paucity of my muscles, whether or not people noticed my misshapen nose (of course they did; it's been busted two times over the years), whether or not I would win the lottery and what plan B would be if I didn't (I needed that money to pay my rent!). I worried about what people thought about me. Did my coworkers think I was smart, funny, witty? For years, I ground my teeth at night so much so that it seemed to me that they looked like little nubbins in my mouth. Adding insult to injury, for years I had suffered as a stutterer. When I went on dates with pretty girls, my mind would go completely blank when I tried to make conversation—I mean John Locke tabula rasa blank. One good thing about worrying is that it makes you creative. For example, I could imagine dozens of different ways I could die in a terrorist attack, but all of those scenarios would evaporate when I tried to engage someone in conversation (upon reflection, I realize that maybe this was a good thing). How I ever got married to the beautiful, normal person who is my wife is undoubtedly a testament to the existence of miracles.

See? I told you I was good at worrying. I have no idea how I dodged a bullet and never got ulcers. Chalk that up to the miraculous.

So some years ago, I was having a beer with a close friend of mine at Croxley's Ale House, a dimly lit local bar known for having fifty different brews on tap. I was worrying out loud about the fact that I worry too much. In response, my friend Eric, a devout Christian who was contemplating converting to Catholicism, suggested that I go on a spiritual retreat. I considered the notion. I wasn't overly enthusiastic about spending a weekend cooped up in a monastery surrounded by people I did not know, praying. To be honest, though I had been raised Catholic and considered myself a rather spiritual person, the whole proposition sounded, well, boring . . . and a little freaky. But the more Eric spoke about his past experiences and the simple acts of devotions and prayers that he engaged in during retreats he had taken, the more convinced I became that there might be some merit to the enterprise. So, after we enjoyed a couple of rounds together, somehow, he persuaded me to give it a shot.

Three weeks later, I found myself at a rather musty old mansion run by an order of Jesuits. Forty other men and I assembled in a brightly lit room known as the solarium, where three walls of floor-to-ceiling windows permitted cascades of natural sunlight to come streaming in. The average age was somewhere between fifty-five and sixty. At the time, I was twenty-six. Surprisingly, most of the men still had hair, although much of it was gray, some Just for Men brown. I saw lots of comfortable walking shoes and flannel shirts. Being a shy person by nature, I sat alone in the back of the room and waited for the leader of the retreat, a priest, to welcome us and deliver his opening remarks.

The priest was running late. I became fidgety. Silently, I was regretting having come on the retreat. Not that I was against praying or anything like that; it's just that I was an impatient twentysomething who would much rather be spending the weekend with my girlfriend, Grace (yes, I had actually found someone who didn't mind my quirks, and we would marry three years later). Plus, when I prayed, I always did so alone. In fact, when I was growing up, the one thing I disliked about going to church was all the people who were around me. I preferred to be by myself and often invoked Jesus's own words as a defense for being antisocial: "But when you pray, go into your room and shut the door and pray to your Father who is in secret" (Matthew 6:6).

Finally, an elderly priest shuffled into the room. He was white haired, tall but hunched over, and seemingly quite frail. *Really?*

This poor guy can barely stand up, let alone speak. Good grief, I thought to myself, with a Charlie Brown cartoon bubble ringing inside my head. I had come to this place to be inspired! I wanted to be motivated! I had anticipated that our retreat leader would be some kind of jacked-up, over-caffeinated Tony Robbins combined with Jesus. I remember scoping out the exit and considering whether anyone would notice if I bolted. And yet, I stayed.

It seemed like it took the priest ten minutes to traverse twenty feet of floor. When he made it to the podium, he just stood there looking down at the papers he was shuffling in front of him. The priest pulled a clean, white handkerchief from his back pocket and dabbed it across his mouth. I noticed that his hand was shaking, as if he might be suffering from Parkinson's disease. He did not make eye contact with anyone in the audience. Then, after another long minute or so of just standing there, he took a deep breath, straightened up (he seemed to grow twelve inches right in front of our eyes), and bellowed in such a loud voice that I nearly fell over in my chair, "HOW BIG IS YOUR GOD?"

The priest was no longer shaking.

"What was *that*?" I said out loud. Being in the back of the room, I don't think anyone heard me. One thing I do know for certain: the solarium, once dull, had become vibrant and alive.

"HOW BIG IS YOUR GOD?" the priest repeated. "IS GOD A SMALL, PETTY GOD WHO GETS MAD AND HOLDS GRUDGES? OR IS GOD A GOD WHO IS THE CREATOR OF THE UNIVERSE, A GOD WHO ACTS BIGGER THAN THE WAY WE DO EVERY DAY? IS GOD A GOD OF VENGEANCE OR IS GOD A FORGIVING GOD? WELL? HOW BIG IS GOD? HUH? HOW BIG IS GOD? IS GOD A HUMAN GOD OR A GODLY GOD?"

Now, I have to explain that at this point the priest wasn't actually yelling. His voice, however, rang out with the timbre of a giant church bell, and I felt as if I were sitting directly under the steeple. Everything seemed to be vibrating. I felt something stir within me. I'm pretty sure that all of us in the solarium were feeling something similar. What was once a quiet place filled with a bunch of sleepy old men now was a room full of something I can only describe as sacred fire.

The priest suggested we meditate on these questions for the remainder of the day and spend our time in devotion to God. With that, he dismissed us. We stood and the other men made their way out of the room. Many were speaking excitedly to one another, as if their tongues had just been blessed. I thought about the Holy Spirit descending upon the apostles. After Christ's death, Jesus's followers retreated to a "large, furnished upper room" (Luke 22:12), where the Last Supper had been celebrated. There they encountered the Holy Spirit, who blessed them with tongues of fire that seemed to hover above their heads. Then, as indeed now, a small multitude of men were "amazed and astonished" (Acts 2:7). Afterward, the apostles were able to go forth and perform miracles. Was this solarium, then, a twentieth-century upper room? I felt a quickening of the flame that had been lit inside me.

I walked up to the podium, where the priest stood shuffling his papers. I noticed that his hands were once again shaking and he seemed to have returned to the same stooped, shrunken size he had been before he rang the bells of our awakening. I asked him a question: "You said spend time in devotion to God. How are we to do that?"

"By loving God. By praising, revering, and serving God. Focus on God's presence in your life," he replied.

"But how do you *do* that? When I think about God I don't feel *any*thing most of the time—just nervous," I confessed.

"It's all about relationship," he replied with equanimity. "Love God. If God is too big for you now, too out of reach, then become devoted to *part* of God, to his sacred heart, maybe. Become devoted to something in the name of God. Care about something. Adore something for God. I don't mean make something an idol, but love something for God the way God loves you."

He paused.

"Even though I just argued that our God should be a big God, sometimes God can be *too* big. If this is how you feel, then try some simple acts of devotion. Pray the Rosary, talk to a saint, read the Bible, meditate on a word, read a holy card. Offer it all up to God."

Then he asked me a question: "You are probably too young to be married, but do you have a girlfriend?"

"Yes," I said. "I do. I think someday I'm going to ask her to marry me."

"Well then, think of all the small things you do for her. Do you buy her a card or bring her flowers or write her a letter? Do you spend time talking to her about your dreams and your fears?"

"Yes, I do all of those things."

"Then do similar things for and with God. It is often the small things that lead us directly to God's heart. It's a big heart."

He looked me in the eyes and once again seemed to grow in stature. "Go pray," he repeated.

"I will," I said, and then I went off to my room to do just that.

What happened next is revealed in the pages that follow.

CHAPTER 2

No Need to Go It Alone

And remember, I am with you always.

—MATTHEW 28:20

In recent years, more and more researchers, doctors, and medical professionals have turned their attention to the study and diagnosis of inflammation, a complex biological reaction in which our bodies naturally attempt to protect themselves from invading pathogens, bacteria, and viruses. Though it often has a negative connotation, inflammation can be a good thing. Scratch yourself on a piece of broken glass and, if you are healthy, your white blood cells will release chemicals to keep harmful substances from entering your bloodstream. Without inflammation, our bodies would not be proficient in healing. And when we don't heal, there can be serious consequences. We could die.

Severe complications often arise, however, when inflammation becomes *chronic*. This condition, studies have shown, can lead to cancer, arthritis, heart attacks, and autoimmune diseases in which our bodies literally turn on themselves, in essence at-

22

tacking normal tissue as if it was a foreign body. Why this happens is not completely understood, though genetics, how we react to stress, and diet and lifestyle seem to play a role. But imagine that you decide to punch yourself hard in the face. And then you do it over and over again until eventually you collapse or knock yourself unconscious. That is what happens when what is supposed to be a natural biological function goes rogue.

What does this have to do with prayer and devotions? Well, just as our bodies can react to injury with a protective process such as inflammation, our souls can react to stress and worry with patterned, habitual responses. We might have an argument with a friend and feel irritated. We may lose a loved one and feel great sadness. We might respond with frustration when a job we loved no longer satisfies an internal yearning for creativity. We may suffer insomnia when we are worried about our finances. In these ways, our feelings and the emotions that arise can be seen as natural responses to the spiritual threats, breaks, punctures, cuts, and bruises we experience as just part of living our lives. In essence, they perform the function of signals that alert us that something is wrong and needs our attention. Just as our bodies might over the course of a few days push out a splinter that is lodged deep in our fingertip, an outburst or a crying spell can help to release pressure around reddened, raw emotions buried deep inside.

These emotional responses are natural. Problems arise, however, not when we feel sadness or disappointment, but when those emotional and spiritual reactions turn chronic, when something inside our minds and hearts turns on itself. This is when it feels as if worry and stress are running the show. Repressed emotions and unacknowledged disappointments can lead to, if you will, arthritis of the soul, in which our minds become rigid, our hearts harden, and we feel stressed out all the time and disconnected from God. Maybe we can't feel joy or satisfaction, or we can't rest. Maybe we feel anxious, fearful, discontented, or angry, or we experience feelings of acedia and malaise, all of which prevent us from loving God and those around us.

I am not a medical professional, nor am I a psychologist. But I have often felt like a refugee in my own soul, lost and confused. However, I have spent the past two decades of my life studying and following spiritual practices. And I have seen and experienced firsthand relief, healing, and transformation with the help of ancient and traditional devotions—simple, sacred prayers, rituals, mysteries, meditations, and small acts of piety that can be done either alone or as a group. For me and for countless millions of others, these spiritual practices have brought solace, healing, and direction during times of trouble and sickness, when all seems lost.

Growing up, I was inconsistent when it came to prayer. Sometimes I prayed with great fervor and other times with the enthusiasm of a sloth. However, ever since my encounter with the priest on that retreat, prayer and devotions have become a sort of second language. One of the ways this new language is expressed is through my constant efforts to see how my everyday experiences can be translated into personal offerings to God. True, I often wish I were more fluent in this language (despite the fact that I have written a number of books on the topic). I have also led workshops on prayer and have worked with children and young adults, introducing them to ancient and contemporary ways of communicating with God. I have prayed in beautiful, Gothic cathedrals off the cobblestone streets of Europe, and I have prayed in potholed parking lots in some of the poorest neighborhoods in the United States. I have hiked to the top of a mountain, leading a group of twenty- and thirtysomethings in prayer and thanksgiving, and I have fasted and prayed in the desert, alone except for a coiled rattlesnake that seemed to watch me from a not-so-comfortable distance. I have attended two exorcisms (truly frightening; I do not recommend), and I have prayed in the presence of angels and saints. Even though my Spanish is rudimentary, I have served in a prayer ministry for a large Hispanic community, performing the act of laying on of hands for dozens of people in the crowded basement of a historic Catholic high school gymnasium every week as I asked God to confer healing and blessings. In prayer circles, I have seen people cry, laugh, collapse, curse, blaspheme, and speak in tongues. And during prayer, I have experienced everything from boredom, frustration, and spiritual dryness to joy, ecstasy, visions, and clairvoyance.

I offer this information not as a sort of spiritual résumé but as an articulation of just how essential and prevalent prayer has been in my life. For many years, I was ignorant of the numerous ways we can draw closer to God. I thought prayer was simply me running off a list of wants, needs, and complaints to the Almighty, as if God was a therapist and I was a client stretched out on a couch and running off at the mouth.

But over time I began a spiritual journey that revealed the diverse, rich, and fascinating method of putting prayerfulness into our lives. I want to share with you some of those experiences and the simple acts that helped me draw closer to God. But before I do that, let's look a little more at what we mean by *devotion*.

CHAPTER 3

The Intelligent Heart

For where your treasure is, there your heart will be also.

—MATTHEW 6:21

Keep your heart with all vigilance, for from it flow the springs of life.

—PROVERBS 4:23

In broad strokes, to be devoted is to place our focused attention on someone or something else. We can be devoted to exercise or an environmental cause. But when Catholics talk about being devoted to Jesus, the Virgin Mary, the holy angels, or to someone such as St. Jude or St. Teresa of Ávila, they are talking about having a very special and committed relationship with the unseen. Devotions are the outward, visible signs of their dedication and affection for God.

Technically, these signs are known as sacramentals, or "little sacraments"—small signs of God's grace. They are customs that have developed over the centuries that aren't part of the ritual you might experience at church on Sundays. Rather, they are demonstrations of the richness and diversity of the Catholic life. Many spiritual traditions found their origin in personal acts of piety, homegrown spiritual practices that eventually grew in popularity among communities of the faithful. Some can date back almost to the time of Jesus. Take, for instance, the Stations of the Cross, a meditation on suffering that emerged from the desire of Christ's earliest followers to reverently trace his steps in the final hours before his death. Over time, more and more people joined in this practice and it spread throughout the Western world. In the early development of this devotion, many would make the pilgrimage to Jerusalem to walk the Via Dolorosa, the Way of Sorrows, to experience the actual sites described in the biblical accounts of Christ's Passion—that is, until the Crusades, when travel to the Holy Land became increasingly perilous. When it became too dangerous for people to make these trips, many churches adapted the walk by constructing artistic images of these events in Jesus's life and placing them on cathedral walls, thereby opening up the practice to locals in a new and much safer way. If this seems a little odd for someone unfamiliar with the practice, consider the memorials in Washington, D.C. that allow tourists the opportunity to honor and connect to people who have given their lives to defend and serve the United States. Many visitors who make pilgrimages to these political memorials speak of them as sacred spaces, monuments of reflection, just like the Stations of the Cross, which can be found in churches all around the world.

Catholic devotions can be prayed silently or recited out loud; some are tactile and go beyond mental exercises by engaging the senses (often with the use of incense or votive candles) or by using strings of beads, badges, pieces of cloth, or small medals that can be found in churches and purchased at religious bookstores.

While there are plenty of devotions we can turn to every day, novenas are some of the most popular and comforting of Catholic spiritual practices. Derived from the Latin word *novem*, which means nine, a novena is a type of devotion recited over nine days. This form of prayer can be used to prepare for a holiday, the birth of a child, or surgery, or it can be used to make a special request to God. A novena can be prayed alone or in a group, in the privacy of your own room or in a church with family and friends. Dozens if not hundreds of different novenas exist. Some are only a couple of sentences and some can go on for pages. More often than not, a novena is used to help with particular intentions. For instance, a novena to St. Jude might be prayed when a loved one is scheduled for a medical operation. The idea is to pray for someone nine days before the event so that the patient is well prepared and well protected for the procedure. Expectant mothers pray novenas in the final days of their pregnancy in anticipation of a safe and easy birth. And many novenas are said for people struggling with everything from addiction to financial crises to an entrance exam for a good school.

But why nine days? Shouldn't a one-day prayer be enough? Especially since, as Jesus taught us, the "Father knows what you need before you ask him" (Matthew 6:8).

Just as a baby needs nine months to grow before it can be born, our prayers often need to gestate in order to be answered. Of course, God can do anything, and he could answer our prayers in the blink of an eye, but novenas help us cultivate a steady prayer life. Just like with healthy eating or exercising, we need to be consistent in our spiritual practice, and novenas can be helpful as reminders to communicate with God every day. Moreover, the number nine has a certain significance in the Bible. It symbolizes completeness and totality. Jesus died in the ninth hour of the day, completing his human mission on earth (until he was resurrected three days later). There are nine charisms, or spiritual gifts, of the Holy Spirit (1 Corinthians 12:28), including wisdom, knowledge, and the power to heal. After Jesus ascended into heaven, Mary and the apostles prayed for nine days in the upper room in anticipation of the Holy Spirit, who descended upon these future saints so that special blessings could be bestowed upon them.

What follows in the sections ahead are prayers to Jesus, Mary, and the saints as well as novenas in honor of God's inimitable holy ones, the angels, that we can make part of our daily lives.

Some of the devotions I cover in this book involve the use of sacramentals such as a scapular or a medal. Originally, a scapular, which finds its origins in the Jewish tallit or prayer shawl, was a narrow piece of cloth worn over the shoulders as part of a religious habit (a garment worn by a member of a religious order—think of the nuns in the movie *The Sound of Music*). Over the centuries this utilitarian cloak, which was supposed to protect the habit from dirt, has morphed into two stamp-size pieces of material connected by ribbon or string that is worn around the neck. Sometimes decorated with symbols—for instance, the popular Brown Scapular of Our Lady of Mount Carmel features an image of Jesus's Sacred Heart and an image of the Blessed Virgin Mary—one piece of cloth sits on the chest and the other lies on the back, a reminder that God is not only right in front of you, leading the way, but also right behind you.

Medals are another type of sacramental. These small pieces of metal or plastic are often inscribed with the visage of Jesus,

Mary, or the saints. They are mini-icons that are usually worn on a chain around the neck, carried in a pocket, wallet, or purse, or even placed in the car or hung from a rearview mirror, as a way of memorializing ideas, people, or visions. One of the most popular, which we will examine more closely later on, is the St. Benedict medal. The medal is inscribed with an image of St. Benedict, founder of the Benedictine order, as well as a secret code in Latin to keep evil and the devil at bay. It is worn not because the object itself has any power but as a reminder and invocation of God's loving triumph over sin and malevolence. While many non-Catholics look at these objects with suspicion—admittedly, they do border on the superstitious if used incorrectly—they are truly intended only to be physical reminders of God's invisible presence. I like to think of them as similar to those devices the elderly wear in case they fall down—just press a button and help is on the way. There are no buttons to press on scapulars and medals, but they are an aide-mémoire to call on God in times of need.

Catholics admittedly love their stuff, and many non-Catholics love to criticize them for such things. We are sometimes accused of being idolaters and pagans by Protestant groups, of being superstitious fools by atheists and agnostics.

Understandable. To those unfamiliar with Catholic practices and rituals, both what we do and the objects we employ in spiritual practice can seem odd. However, seen from another point of view, it is precisely the unusual nature of these customs and ceremonies that takes us out of our ordinary, material existence and places us in the midst of something that is out of this world even as it is fully present in the world at all times.

And while we don't really need a medal or the light of a candle to pray, these tools serve a purpose by helping us to focus. Human beings are physical creatures. We like touch. We like to feel things, see things. We are inherently and simultaneously artists and lovers of art, whether or not we are conscious of this attribute. Devotions such as the Rosary allow us to engage our senses during prayer. Ultimately, tapping into all of our senses can open pathways from the head to the heart.

Moreover, human beings are a forgetful lot. Think about how often we misplace our keys or can't recall the names of people we meet at parties. Items that are associated with devotions are like the string that our grandparents tied around their fingers to remind them to do something, or the alert that buzzes on our phones before a meeting. They are reminders of God's presence. They remind us to follow the Ten Commandments and to be kind to others. They cue us that we are protected by a force greater than any other.

Now, some of you might be skeptical. That's understandable. We live in a world that is suspicious of devotion in all its forms. The media constantly bombards us with stories and images of people who are devoted to, for example, extremism, or greed. We know that devotion to militant religious ideology can lead to war, chaos, and destruction. Psychologists and therapists may assert that devotion to another person is unhealthy, perhaps even a sign of codependency or low self-esteem. These are valid considerations that demonstrate how dedication to an idea, a cause, or a person can sometimes go awry. But when I speak of devotion, I am not talking about religious fanaticism; rather, I am talking of the "God is love" kind of relationship we read about in the Bible. God isn't *like* love or *kinda like* love. God *is* love. And if someone is truly devoted to God then ipso facto that person is devoted to love. To again quote the Bible, "Love is patient, love is kind. It does

not envy, it does not boast, it is not proud. It does not dishonor others, it is not self-seeking, it is not easily angered, it keeps no record
of wrongs. Love does not delight in evil but rejoices with the truth.
It always protects, always trusts, always hopes, always perseveres.
Love never fails" (1 Corinthians 13:4–8). Devotion is not the act of
blowing people up or shooting men and women in a nightclub in,
as we have heard far too often, the name of God. True acts of devotion are true acts of love, compassion, mercy, and forgiveness.

Yet, we live in a strange time when truth and lies are mixed
together in a dangerous cocktail that causes confusion, frustration, and anger. More and more of us feel like we don't belong to
anything anywhere. We hear that millions of people each year are
leaving their religion behind. But for what? Our individual faith
often feels weak; our purpose, ambiguous. Collectively, we feel
like wanderers, lost and unsatisfied by modern ideas about what
it means to be truly human. The words of W. B. Yeats's poem "The
Second Coming" feel terribly prescient:

> *Turning and turning in the widening gyre*
> *The falcon cannot hear the falconer;*
> *Things fall apart; the center cannot hold;*
> *Mere anarchy is loosed upon the world,*
> *The blood-dimmed tide is loosed, and everywhere*
> *The ceremony of innocence is drowned;*
> *The best lack all conviction; while the worst*
> *Are full of passionate intensity.*

What are we to do?

Often when we find ourselves lost, anxious, and nervous
about where we are going, it is best to stop, survey the landscape,

and turn around. Retrace our steps. Over the years, this has meant, for me, a return to tradition. When the world seems to have forgotten the past, what could be more countercultural than getting back to basics?

Devotions function as a tap on the shoulder, a way of reorienting our soul's journey to the divine. They not only help us know God better, but they help us know God's beloved son, Jesus, better and in different ways. Maintaining a devotion to St. Jude is like cultivating a friendship with one of Jesus's best friends, a man who knew certain things about Jesus that others did not, one of Jesus's apostles who witnessed miracles and healings right before his very eyes. To have a devotion to the holy angels is to develop an intimate friendship with our heavenly hosts, and in that relationship, Jesus is revealed to us in ways St. Jude never experienced. Perhaps the angels can tell us more about their relationship with God the Father, or with the Holy Spirit. So too is a devotion to the Virgin Mary something entirely unique; here, since it is about building a relationship with the mother of Jesus, certain things can be revealed to us that are particular to her relationship with him. Mary can let us know what he was like as a child or a teenager with a kind of intimacy Jesus's friends and the public never knew.

A warning: placing our focus only on the practice itself or on a particular saint can lead to idolatry, which is why it is understandable that critics of devotions might express skepticism about the practice. If we forget that the saints are our friends and helpers and instead look to them as having some kind of supernatural power in and of themselves, then we have taken our attention off Jesus. In the movie *Enter the Dragon*, Bruce Lee instructs a student that the ineffable is like "a finger pointing to the moon." He then chides another student, smacking him on the head, for focusing on the finger. "Don't focus on the finger or you'll miss all that heavenly glory." The point here is that the one question we should always be asking when it comes to our spiritual practice is, "Does this lead me to Jesus?" If it doesn't, then reconsider the act.

The saints can help guide us. In the opening scenes of *The Divine Comedy*, the poet Dante experiences a heavenly vision and tries to ascend a mountain with his own abilities, using his wits and insight. He soon discovers that there are barriers that block his way to God. He can't ascend until he finds a guide, and even then he has to backtrack and relearn so much of what he thinks he knows. The more Dante is exposed to the truths of God and Jesus, the more his thinking about himself changes and the easier his path becomes, until eventually he is given a true vision of what it means to experience God. It comes to him in the beauty of a heavenly rose. No longer is a rose just a rose; for Dante, it becomes a manifestation of God's love and magnificence. Get to know Jesus better and your life will no longer be your own, but an expression of life everlasting.

On my writing desk is a little picture that a friend of mine sent me. The caption reads, "The sooner you turn back, the quicker you can get on the right path." This gift shop sentiment contains a world of truth. Prayers and devotions give us the opportunity to turn back, to shift our focus from ourselves to Jesus, from our problems to God's plan for us, which when you're suffering or challenged can seem a world away. Being in the presence of God, the Holy Spirit, Jesus, the saints, or the angels is enough to transform us. Just as being in sunlight changes the color of our skin and affects us down to the cellular level, being in the pure light of the Divine can also change us from our surface to our core. Yet, just as we won't get a suntan if we hide out in a closet all day, we cannot become radiant unless we place ourselves in the presence of the Divine.

Part II

The Path

*Prepare your work outside; get everything ready for
yourself in the field, and after that, build your house.*

—PROVERBS 24:27

CHAPTER 4

Step 1: Be Childlike

*Down on the lake rosy reflections of celestial vapor ap-
peared, and I said, "God, I love you" and looked to the sky
and really meant it. "I have fallen in love with you, God.
Take care of us all, one way or the other." To the children
and the innocent it's all the same.*

—JACK KEROUAC, *THE DHARMA BUMS*

I remember a few weeks after my oldest son started kindergarten
I took him one late Indian summer afternoon to the St. Ignatius
Retreat House in Manhasset, New York. This eighty-seven-room,
72,000-square-foot Tudor Elizabethan mansion, where I first met
Father How Big Is Your God, was a jewel of the legendary Gold
Coast of the 1920s. Once the summerhouse for devout Catholics
Nicholas and Genevieve Brady, the manor sported ornate brick-
work complete with gargoyles and bas-reliefs of fairy tales such as
Little Red Riding Hood, and more than one dozen towering chim-
neys that pointed straight up to heaven. Over the years this couple, undoubtedly members of the New York elite, donated millions

to charity and even hosted such Church legends as Bishop Fulton Sheen, Cardinal Francis Spellman, and Vatican Secretary of State Cardinal Eugenio Pacelli, who would later become Pope Pius XII. Nicknamed Inisfada (a Gaelic word for Long Island), the stately house and opulent grounds were eventually bequeathed by the Bradys to the Jesuits, who turned it into an unofficial park for anyone looking to stroll through the beautiful thirty-three acres that surrounded the house, as well as a haven for those in need of spiritual direction. For my son and me, both Harry Potter fans, this estate became a real-life Hogwarts, a place of mystery and imagination—quite the contrast from the cookie-cutter homes and strip malls that line a large part of the suburban landscape east of New York City.

Shy in front of strangers, though rambunctious and funny in front of his family, Eddie, four years old at the time, had been struggling in kindergarten, finding it difficult to acclimate to his classroom and all the students he saw every day. Truth be told, he was suffering a mild case of separation anxiety and simply missed his home and his mom, feelings many kids have at that age. But as much as we thought he was a great and smart kid, Eddie proved not to be a favorite of his teacher or his principal. Both of them had choice words for us as parents for not having sent Eddie to pre-K to "develop the skills he needed to interact with students and teachers." (Well, you do not say anything like that to my fiery Sicilian wife, who refused to reveal to the school that she had been an educator herself for more than ten years and had schooled our son at home and through various library programs. "Who do they think they are?" she fumed. Who did they think they were, indeed! But that is a story for another time.)

Ever since I took Eddie to Inisfada a year earlier, the lush grounds, with tall oaks, gravel pathways, canopied trails, gurgling stream, and stone labyrinth, had been a land of adventure and exploration for the two of us. We would take plastic swords (sometimes Star Wars lightsabers) and seek out villains to be fought and monsters to be conquered. The vilest of these imaginary creatures was the dreaded Minotaur, half man, half bull, who was trapped somewhere inside a maze of rock that lay just beyond the mansion. Often Eddie was Theseus the Brave and I was the grotesque monster in search of a hero to devour.

Today, however, we had no swords, only sticks. I knighted Eddie St. George the Dragon Slayer and we spent the afternoon in search of an imaginary flying serpent. Once we discovered and then vanquished it, we carried the make-believe beast to the base of a six-foot-tall statue of the Virgin Mary that stood atop a small incline on the north end of the property. "For you, Our Lady, Slayer of Serpents yourself." We spent much of the rest of our time exploring the estate, playing hide-and-go-seek, running along the outer edge of the perimeter, up hills and through vegetation, and we tossed small pebbles into a pond that lay beneath the protection of an unnamed Greek goddess. After the stresses of the previous week at school, the afternoon proved to be restorative and empowering not only for my son but for me as well, as I would be going back to my own fray at work on Monday morning.

As the day turned to dusk, beneath a copper-and-blue crepuscular sky we made our way down a hill toward an enormous weeping beech tree, where bull beasts and angry dragons were known to hide.

Sticks in hand, we entered a cavernous enclosure created by the drooping branches and suddenly found ourselves inside a world of shadows and shade. We clambered over thick exposed roots and crooked, yearning branches that looked like witch fingers beckoning us to draw closer to the trunk of the tree. I kept my hand near Eddie's back to catch him if he lost his footing. We talked about Mario Bros and dinosaurs and we played a quick pickup game of stickball with the large beechnuts that littered the dark ground.

Dusk turned to evening and I told my son it was time to go. As we exited this tree castle, a quarter moon struggled to shine in the east and the blue hill before us looked murky and desolate. We were entirely alone except for a light shining in the window of an upper room in the mansion some distance away. I reached out and took Eddie's hand and we walked together. We stopped for a moment. I wanted to feel the air on my face and stand beneath the vast sky above us. And that is when my son said, "Daddy, I'm afraid. Don't let go of my hand."

I looked at Eddie, squeezed my fingers into his tiny palm, and said, "Don't be afraid. I'll always be with you." He gave my hand a squeeze in return and kept close to my side as we walked in silence through a pale path cut by the dull light of the moon. We made our way to the parking lot, climbed into the family car, and headed home.

My son is older now and he no longer holds my hand when we go for walks. Inisfada and the enchanted landscape that was our playground were demolished a few years ago when the Jesuits sold the property to an investment firm looking to build condos (I know that God asks us to be forgiving, yet certain things seem to me to be a little bit unforgivable). But when I think back to that night I realize that in that singular moment, Eddie helped me experience and understand the purest and most innocent form of prayer: "Daddy, I'm afraid. Don't let go of my hand." The spirit of Eddie's words is arguably at the center of every single honest prayer and the first step to the devotional life: *I need you, God; stay with me.*

In other words, surrender and be open to God's ability to help and protect you.

We live in a time and place that stresses independence and individualism, self-reliance and self-worth. To rely on another is to put oneself in a precarious position. But long before psychologists coined terms such as *codependency* and before theologians intellectualized prayer and concocted new names for the way we communicate with God, somewhere, one quivering, frightened person looked up at the sky and asked an invisible presence to help him feel less alone.

"Because you are his children, God sent the Spirit of his Son into our hearts, the Spirit who calls out, 'Abba, Father'" (Galatians 4:6).

Father, Abba, I am afraid; stay with me.

HONEST TO GOD

Now, many of us might not want to admit some of the motivations behind our prayers to God. Someone might say, "I pray because I want to get to know God better," or "I want to give thanks for my blessings." That's admirable, but most of us aren't that brave. We often feel lonely, sad, dejected, threatened, and frightened by the circumstances of life. We need reassurance that we are not alone, that we are protected, but many of us feel embarrassed to admit that we are afraid, that our feelings get hurt, that we are vulnerable. Instead of being frank, we try to protect our-

selves from our emotions. We close off our hearts. We intellectu-
alize what we are feeling. We begin creating mental movies of
our fears—horror films, if you will—and project them onto the
interior screens of our minds, watching them nonstop, like our
own personal Netflix marathon. Anyone who has sat in front of
a TV, computer screen, or video game console watching electronic
images flash for hours and hours knows the erratic, nervous feeling it can create. Think of what we do to ourselves when we can't
turn off the internal movies and allow them to run 24-7. We become anxious beyond our capacity to process anxiety, and when
there is too much tension in anything, eventually some part of that
thing will snap.

Our unexpressed fears often create spiritual and mental pressure cookers that if not handled properly can become quite dangerous. The overflow of energy can lead to chronic anxiety,
insomnia, and depression. We often trick ourselves into thinking
that God doesn't know what we are experiencing. We might be
uneasy about an aging parent; we could be worried that our jobs
are in jeopardy because of outsourcing; we are distraught over an
impending separation or divorce; we are fearful that we can't pay
our bills; we struggle with self-doubt, sickness, disease, and life-
changing injuries. Whatever it is we are facing, many of us attempt to put on a brave face and kid ourselves and everyone
around us that we are doing fine, even though we are essentially
scared out of our minds.

One of the first things to be aware of while preparing to pray
is to enter devotion with an honest heart, to be vulnerable. Just
tell God how we feel. Not what we think—what we feel. Lay our
fears and concerns on God's shoulders. By this I do not mean

whine like people playing out roles on reality TV shows, but actually express to God what is going on inside us. Confide in him. Share as if to our very best friend all of our dreams, doubts, worries, and uncertainties. There is no reason to feel like an outsider when we are living in a world created just for us by our very best friend.

CHAPTER 5

Step 2: Focus Your Mind and Heart

Blessed are the pure in heart, for they shall see God.

—MATTHEW 5:8

And now here is my secret, a very simple secret: It is only with the heart that one can see rightly; what is essential is invisible to the eye.

—ANTOINE DE SAINT-EXUPÉRY, *THE LITTLE PRINCE*

Many of us have heard the suggestion that if we change our thoughts, we can change our lives. Or that there is an infinite intelligence upon which we can draw for inspiration and strength, a force that can solve all our problems. We may have heard words such as *Godhead* or been introduced to philosophical and theological principles that refer to God as the divine mind. We hold great thinkers and thought leaders in high esteem. We're told that if we can just have faith in our own thoughts, then our prayers can come true. Many believe that if we think the right way we can grow rich materially and spiritually. Moreover, we are urged to practice mindfulness in our daily lives—to pay attention to what we are thinking and be present in the now.

These are admirable ideas and concepts, and each contains some level of truth. Our minds are powerful instruments; all of our experiences *seem* to begin in our thoughts. The paths of our lives are often determined by whether those thoughts are positive or negative. Consider the positive thinking of two people in love who want to create a family and experience the joy that can come from the birth of their children. Or imagine a man who dreams of creating a hospital to serve those with the direst of needs. Consider also the negative thinking of dictators and criminals who have no problem inflicting pain and destruction upon those around them. Think of the brilliance of Einstein's $E = mc^2$ and the destructive power of Oppenheimer's "destroyer of worlds" bomb born from that equation. Thoughts certainly are things that can raise us up or tear us down. Ideas are behind computers and bridges just as they are behind the actions of terrorists and killers. Ideas shape the way people love and hate. Ideas can inspire life-saving technologies at the same time as they can instigate murderous rampages.

Yet, this emphasis we have put on our thoughts seems to be a product born of left-brain thinking. Our intellects, however, are only part of who we are. Why do we not praise great heart leaders, or try to access infinite emotion? Why are we not told that a change of heart will change our lives? Why don't we hear more often that we should meditate on the Godheart? And could we *feel* and grow rich instead of always *thinking* about everything?

Truth be told, our heads are often terrible translators of what's going on inside us. Sometimes when we feel upset emotionally our brains tell us to grab something unhealthy to eat. We might feel nervous and our brains tell us that we should smoke a cigarette. We might feel lost or disinterested and our brains say, Hey, let's start an argument with someone, or, Let's waste hours of time surfing the Internet. We feel tired and our brains lash out at someone we love. We feel bored in a relationship so our brains say, Go find love somewhere else. It's as if something inside us is throwing up roadblocks, creating detours for natural impulses that only lead to dead-end behavior. Our minds, of course, are the culprits, which is why there have been so many books published over the past ten years about mindfulness, about paying attention to our thoughts and attempting to quiet their bratty behaviors.

Yet, many of these books and ideas stop before they get to the really good stuff. When we can quiet the mind, which is often a chatterbox, then our heart, which is often more soft-spoken, can be heard. The heart may very well be the origin of our intelligence. The ancients intuited this. Egyptians believed the heart was the center of thought and the entry point to the afterlife; to weigh the heart was to determine whether or not you would live forever. The Bible itself uses the word *heart* nearly a thousand times. Again, the heart was considered the hub of thinking, the origin of all being. Knowing their thoughts, Jesus said, "Why do you entertain evil thoughts in your hearts?" (Matthew 9:4).

The ancients knew what science has confirmed, namely that in an embryo the heart makes its first appearance by day eighteen of gestation. The brain doesn't show up until two weeks later. The first organ to function is the heart. It's as if an intelligence inside this cardiac muscle is sending information to the brain. This might sound like science fiction, but more and more researchers now believe that the heart is constantly in dialogue with the brain, sending twice as many electrical signals to the brain than the brain sends to the heart.

All our experiences carry with them some form of emotional resonance. A meeting at work may make us feel nervous, we may feel slighted by a loved one and react by feeling sad, and sometimes we feel anger when things don't go our way. More often than not our minds rush to the scene of the incident and start blabbering about what all of this can mean. Our brains really aren't geared toward thinking as much as they're designed to keep us alive, to protect us from threats. What happens is that all the chatter drowns out the still, quiet voice of the heart, which actually knows what should be done. In the end, our feelings are suppressed. Our mind takes over like an obnoxious guest at a dinner party, the one who just won't shut up.

All of these experiences—from arguments to broken hearts to financial problems to our health—are invitations to grow closer to God by allowing our center to be in conversation with his. Moreover, we can see another side to feelings of discontent, malaise, and isolation; they can either get us down or they can be seen as a kick in the pants to shift our focus to the Almighty.

What I am saying here is that we should not approach prayer as if it's an intellectual exercise. Prayer should come from the heart. Failing to try to understand how our emotions can be bridges to God disregards an important part of who we are. And when we lose sight of this miracle of connection, we miss out on extraordinary spiritual truths that affect our day-to-day lives.

At first blush, devotions, which are the music and songs of the mystics, might seem archaic and old-fashioned, mere vestiges or decrepit relics of bygone generations, fodder for sweet gray-haired old ladies with too much time on their hands. An example of a widespread superstition is the belief that carrying a St. Benedict medal can keep the devil away. This is the kind of well-practiced way of imploring saints for help that keeps scholars and theologians away from the topic. Like UFOs and Bigfoot, saints might appear to be remnants of wishful thinking engaged in by people who felt helpless to influence what was going on in their culture. But, to borrow a line from Hamlet, "There are more things in heaven and Earth, Horatio, than are dreamt of in your philosophy." I would agree with Shakespeare. There most surely is more here than meets the eye.

Devotions appeal not to the intellect but to the heart. They are not exercises in mindfulness; they are experiences of heartfulness. In their simplicity, in their innocent and tactile nature, they give the head some time to rest from all its questioning and analyzing. They appeal instead to the creative, artistic, and emotional nature of our beings. If many of the great theologians such as St. Thomas Aquinas, St. Augustine, and Edith Stein were left-brainers—that is to say, intelligent men and women who were able to analyze and unpack the meaning and significance of a passage in the Bible with brilliance—then mystics such as St. John of the Cross, St. Bernadette, and Teresa of Ávila, with their focus on visions, emotions, and sensory experience, can be seen as consummate right-brainers, or, intuitive people who favor imagination over logic.

Devotion is the turning of our deepest selves to God. It is not the ears but the heart that hears the song of life everlasting. It is drawn to the eternal the way our bodies yearn for the warmth and light of the sun after the cold, gray days of winter. We can feel it upon waking in the moments before our minds start racing with our endless to-do lists, grievances, concerns, and worries. There, in the silence, as the darkness of night gives way to the dawn of morning, we feel something stir in us: the urgency of love, the passion for connection, the wordless dreams. This doesn't last for long. Once the mind realizes we are awake, it turns on us like a jealous lover and puts the heart under house arrest, locking us in a room where we can only peek out of windows, preventing us from going outside and experiencing something greater.

Leading a devotional life is ultimately about leading a sensory and experiential life. An example: I can read all about the Korean martial art tae kwon do—the techniques, philosophy, and history—but still not be able to launch a kick correctly. I actually need to perform, to move my body in a certain way and feel the pain that is a consequence of moving my leg incorrectly in contrast to the pleasure of proper execution, and I need to practice basic forms in order to gain any proficiency in the discipline. The same holds true for God. Though we can gain insight about what he is like, we can't truly experience God by reading, thinking, or hearing about him. We can only know God through experience, and we experience him uniquely when we pray from the heart, when we honestly reach out and, with the spirit of a child, slip our hand into his and say, "I'm afraid. Don't let go of me."

This is not to say that we should neglect the intellect in our lives, prayers, and devotions. In our day-to-day experiences we need to be educated and informed, we need to use critical thinking and practice the art of making good decisions. We live in a real world with real demands and very real consequences. True religion and true spirituality isn't about being a dummy, but neither is it about being a scholar. It's just that so very often the mind gets in the way. Do atheists *feel* that there is no God, or do they *think* there's no God? Jesus's apostles weren't professors or scribes; they were people who worked with their hands, who did the dirty work of everyday life—fishermen and tradesmen who smelled of sea and sweat. Our thoughts about God can inch us closer to experience with him, but a PhD in philosophy doesn't mean you know God any better than does a frail Italian woman with her shawl and rosary beads chanting a litany of Hail Marys in the back of the church. Often that woman knows more about God than entire schools of smarty-pants who are convinced that they have everything figured out.

So the second step before we enter devotion is to pay attention to our thoughts *and* our feelings. When we do this, we begin moving in the direction of wholeness, toward a marriage of the head and the heart.

CHAPTER 6

Step 3: Make the Sign

When, then, you make the sign of the cross on the forehead,
arm yourself with a saintly boldness, and reinstall your
soul in its old liberty; for you are not ignorant that the cross
is a prize beyond all price.

—ST. JOHN CHRYSOSTOM

The sign of the cross is how Catholics begin and end every prayer. It's an invocation, a preparatory rite, a way of creating sacred space. It's a physical gesture in which we touch our foreheads with the fingertips of our right hand and intone, "In the name of the Father." We then move down toward our chest and say, "and the Son." Then we move the hand from our left shoulder to our right shoulder while saying the words, "and the Holy Spirit." The invocation then ends with bringing both hands together with an "Amen."

You've seen Sylvester Stallone bless himself in the Rocky movies just as the bell rings and the fighting commences. You see football players make the sign as they are about to receive a punt or just after they've scored a touchdown. You might catch sight of a family quietly making the sign before eating a meal in a restaurant. It is a blessing that we bestow upon ourselves as well as an invitation for the Holy Spirit to be present in our meditations and in our lives. Moreover, the sign of the cross is a symbol of the sacred, of the life-giving nature of Jesus. It is a mark of Christ's victory over death, and, like many prayers, it has its own supernatural power. It is used during the holy Mass and the rites of baptism and marriage, and even during exorcism, as a physical, spiritual reminder of the extraordinary power of God's grace.

Yet, for most of my life the sign of the cross was something I performed rather mindlessly at the beginning and end of church services. It had little significance for me. I sometimes rushed through it as if I was wiping something off my face and body. Now I take my time. I've come to see that the sign of the cross is both a blessing as well as a road map to the devotional life. *Road map?* you ask. *How so?* Let me explain.

Most of us begin our prayers by coming in contact with our heads—that is to say, with our intellect—symbolized here as the Father and centered in the forehead. We may read, study, and pray intensely. We may meditate for long hours trying to get our minds to slow down, or we may exchange ideas with one another about what it means to be a spiritual person. This is all well and good, but it is only the first stop on the road of our spiritual journey. At a certain point, we have to leave behind the intellect and move to the place of the heart—the place of emotion and sensation, where there are no words, just these sensations and emotions. We move to the heart precisely because this is the symbol of the Son, Jesus. This is the place of experience. But even then, just as in the sign, our journey through the spiritual life isn't complete. We still have to surrender to our experiences, whether those are a birth, a death, a change in jobs, or an upsetting encounter of some kind, and allow the heart to be pierced by the Holy Spirit—all of which is signified in the movement of the right hand from the left shoulder to the right shoulder. It is a moment when we encounter an enormous God who is greater than our collective intellects and grander than all our hearts. It is this acknowledgment of mind, heart, and spirit that leads to the great affirmation of life, the amen, a word that means "so be it."

The sign of the cross, therefore, is a potent reminder to engage both our minds and our hearts as best we can in our prayers to honor not only the Father but also the Son. Making the sign is a beckoning to think and reflect, to feel and to ponder.

Yet, as human beings, our own efforts can only take us so far. We then need to surrender our prayers to the Holy Spirit to work its grace in our lives. In other words, do the best you can—the absolute best you can—and then don't worry about the outcome. When we do this, the sign of the cross is converted from a physical gesture to a blessing. We are blessed by God when we can allow our full being to be present in our prayers and in everything we do in our lives.

One of the most important words in the sign of the cross is *and*. We invoke the Father *and* the Son *and* the Holy Spirit. Our devotional life is not an either-or existence. Rather, it is one governed by the holy *and*. We are body *and* soul, flesh *and* spirit, mind *and* heart, human *and* divine, sinners *and* saints, visible *and* invisible, transient *and* eternal. We are by our very nature a collection of paradoxes, and the specifics of our devotional life are no different, made up of church and private prayer, community and solitude, words and emotions, light and shadow, which ultimately leads to the experience of heaven and earth in the here and now.

This is all well and good, but what does it mean on a practical basis? Simply this: Think about what is being prayed for. Listen to the words that are being spoken. Engage your mind and ask yourself what meaning these words have, how they apply in your life. And then quiet your mind. Give it a rest. Allow the words to penetrate all the way into your heart.

One of the easiest ways to relax the mind is to breathe rhythmically and envision the words of the prayer peacefully moving from forehead to heart. We can close our eyes and picture the actual words on the screens of our minds as they travel down our heads, necks, and trunks until they come to rest in our hearts. And then we let the words take up residence right there, trying our best to allow them to be present in the seat of our emotions. What we are striving to accomplish with this preparation is the making of a receptacle that will accept without judgment what we need to talk about with God. Our hearts should be appreciated as a safe place where the relationship between God and us will be cherished, honored, and protected. We can even physically touch our heart area with our hands as if we are placing the words into our hearts.

CHAPTER 7

Step 4: Say the Lord's Prayer

Pray then in this way.

—MATTHEW 6:9

After we begin our devotion with the sign of the cross, we should recite the Lord's Prayer. Why? Well, there are many reasons. It's a simple prayer, it's how Jesus taught us to pray, and it instantly shifts our focus to heavenly things; all devotions should lead us back to God and Jesus. It is also a way of purifying ourselves. The Lord's Prayer is like hand sanitizer for the soul. It's a prayer of praise and humility, of petition and forgiveness. As C. S. Lewis was known to say, and I am paraphrasing, we wash our hands before we eat—shouldn't we also clean our souls before entering into prayer? Moreover, embedded in the Lord's Prayer are six levels of awareness that we should keep in our hearts in our day-to-day devotional lives.

Our Father, who art in heaven, hallowed be thy name

In other words, praise God.

This part of the prayer is about acknowledging God, the Creator of the universe, who is ultimately responsible for the sun and the moon and the seas and the mountains; God, the ancient of days and the Most High responsible for our universe, the planets and stars, for dark matter and dark energy and the laws of physics, for kittens and dinosaurs, for blues and jazz, and the Renaissance and board games and children and you and me. It is about honoring God, praising God. I can barely create a ball out of Play-Doh, so when I look around and I see all the individuals, the art, the buildings, the nature that originated from God's command—let there be light, let there be life—I am struck by a sense of wonder and awe. We should not be afraid to cultivate that awe. We should not be afraid to express it the way Jesus does here. He praises his Father. So should we.

Thy kingdom come, thy will be done, on earth as it is in heaven

In other words, be humble.

God made us to be cocreators, to do what he did at the dawn of time except on a lesser, humbler scale. We can make a skyscraper, but God, using erosion and the passage of time, can make the Grand Canyon. It is our job to assist in creating heaven on earth. We accept that. But, like fallen angels, we can make choices that create situations that are antithetical to God's kingdom. Be conscious that God's kingdom is one of beauty rather than conflict. We are called to humble ourselves to God's will, but are told that whatever he wills in heaven can be willed on earth. We'll go into this more later, but the idea here is to acknowledge God's will even as we know that we can petition him for change.

Give us this day our daily bread

In other words, make the request.

We shouldn't be afraid to ask God to feed us physically, mentally, spiritually, and psychologically. We should humbly request the things we need—food, clothing, shelter, love, companionship, stable communities. We can also ask God for the things we want, but we should start with what we *need* to create a life in which we can pursue the desires that will help us better serve God and all of creation.

And forgive us our trespasses as we forgive those
who trespass against us

In other words, live in a perpetual state of asking for forgiveness.

No matter how good we think we are in our lives, it's a given that we probably screwed up something on any particular day, whether we forgot to acknowledge the checkout person with a sincere greeting, were impatient with our children, spouse, or coworker, or passed a homeless person on the street without even making eye contact. Before any devotion, then, always ask for forgiveness. Our Father will forgive us, and he expects us to forgive others as well. Don't hold grudges. Ironically, the one thing in the Bible that God seems to find unforgivable is for us not to forgive others.

> Then Peter approaching asked him, "Lord, if my brother
> sins against me, how often must I forgive him? As many
> as seven times?" Jesus answered, "I say to you, not seven

times but seventy-seven times. That is why the kingdom of heaven may be likened to a king who decided to settle accounts with his servants. When he began the accounting, a debtor was brought before him who owed him a huge amount. Since he had no way of paying it back, his master ordered him to be sold, along with his wife, his children, and all his property, in payment of the debt. At that, the servant fell down, did him homage, and said, 'Be patient with me, and I will pay you back in full.' Moved with compassion the master of that servant let him go and forgave him the loan. When that servant had left, he found one of his fellow servants who owed him a much smaller amount. He seized him and started to choke him, demanding, 'Pay back what you owe.' Falling to his knees, his fellow servant begged him, 'Be patient with me, and I will pay you back.' But he refused. Instead, he had him put in prison until he paid back the debt. Now when his fellow servants saw what had happened, they were deeply disturbed, and went to their master and reported the whole affair. His master summoned him and said to him, 'You wicked servant! I forgave you your entire debt because you begged me to. Should you not have had pity on your fellow servant, as I had pity on you?' Then in anger his master handed him over to the torturers until he should pay back the whole debt. So will my heavenly Father do to you, unless each of you forgives his brother from his heart." (Matthew 18:21–35)

Is that threat at the end similar to a threat a parent might give her child, knowing full well she'd never act on it? We don't know for sure, so it seems pretty clear that we should definitely just forgive!

And lead us not into temptation

In other words, don't be stupid.

This is so important in our devotional lives. We should always ask God to steer us away from temptation. We should never, ever ask to be put to the test, for we have no idea what we might be asking for. We should never challenge God or throw down a gauntlet as if to say, "I can handle anything you throw at me." We should not tempt fate. Arrogance can often lead us down dark paths.

But deliver us from evil.

Yes, evil exists in many forms. Don't think it doesn't.

To reiterate, never, ever put God to the test. To do so demonstrates a lack of humility that is an invitation for evil to enter. As illustrated when the devil is trying to tempt Jesus in the desert:

> Then the devil took him up to a very high mountain, and showed him all the kingdoms of the world in their magnificence, and he said to him, "All these I shall give to you, if you will prostrate yourself and worship me." At this, Jesus said to him, "Get away, Satan! It is written:
>   'The Lord, your God, shall you worship
>   and him alone shall you serve.'"
> Then the devil left him and, behold, angels came and ministered to him. (Matthew 4:8–11)

In our often fractured and hurting world, the powers that be are frequently putting us to the test. In turn we should constantly be asking God to deliver us from the evil that is always around us in big and small ways.

Finally, finish with *Amen*, or so be it.

So be it.

CHAPTER 8

Step 5: Ask, Seek, Knock

Ask and it will be given to you; seek and you will find; knock and the door will be opened for you. For everyone who asks receives, and everyone who searches finds, and for everyone who knocks, the door will be opened.

—MATTHEW 7:7–8

Jesus prays often in the Gospels—at parties, on the street, at dinner, in the desert, and on mountains. He prays with others and while he's alone, often retiring to deserted places to be alone with God. We see him praying for the sick and the dead and for children and women, which is very significant. During the first century, Palestinian women and children were viewed as property and often not worthy of prayer. Jesus saw past these labels, viewing every person as a creature of God. He taught by example that prayer isn't a onetime event, something we do halfheartedly. We need to be persistent in prayer, as he tells his followers in the parable of the persistent widow (Luke 18:1–8):

Then Jesus told them a parable about their need to pray always and not to lose heart. He said, "In a certain city there was a judge who neither feared God nor had respect for people. In that city there was a widow who kept coming to him and saying, 'Grant me justice against my opponent.' For a while he refused; but later he said to himself, 'Though I have no fear of God and no respect for anyone, yet because this widow keeps bothering me, I will grant her justice, so that she may not wear me out by continually coming.'" And the Lord said, "Listen to what the unjust judge says. And will not God grant justice to his chosen ones who cry to him day and night? Will he delay long in helping them? I tell you, he will quickly grant justice to them. And yet, when the Son of Man comes, will he find faith on earth?"

Jesus prayed for rejects, lepers, and losers. And when he prayed, healings occurred, storms were calmed, demons were expelled, and the dead came back to life.

Now, Jesus prays effectively, but many of us might be thinking, He's God, so his prayers seem to have an advantage over those of mere mortals. I know I've prayed for a headache to go away and it just lingers and lingers.

But maybe that advantage isn't as big as it might seem. Jesus says outright, "Therefore I tell you, whatever you ask in prayer, believe that you have received it, and it will be yours" (Mark 11:24). If Jesus is the Way, the Truth, and the Life, then he isn't lying. He's telling us the God's honest truth. We have the power for our petitions to be this effective too. So why do so many of our requests seemingly go unanswered?

No one can give a definitive answer. Often prayers go unanswered because the answered prayer that we are looking for might not be good for us or for the people around us. If someone wants to make some quick cash and prays for a giant bag of crack and the crack doesn't materialize, then maybe God is saying, "Um, you might want to get your priorities straight." Think of a mom putting the kibosh on her fourteen-year-old son's request for beer at his birthday party. Her life is motivated by a desire to make her child happy, but she knows this request is not appropriate and can lead to disaster.

Even some of Jesus's prayers weren't answered in the way he wanted. Three times he called out to his father in the Garden of Gethsemane, asking God to halt the pain and suffering he was anticipating. Well, we know how that turned out. Yet, with the Resurrection, that unanswered prayer turned out to be a blessing not only for Jesus but also for the whole world.

So even though praying is not a surefire bet, Jesus urges us to do so and he gives us a couple of ways that can help us unfold our devotional life.

Often we are looking for the newest appliance, car, computer, or phone. We seem to have a default setting that tells us new is better, but when it comes to prayer, we would be better served if we got back to the old, traditional ways. Ask, seek, knock seems basic enough. We ask God for what we want, whether this is better health, world peace, or to discover our purpose in life. But he doesn't just want us to hang around and do nothing. We pray and then we seek God as the motivating force in the world around us. Where, for example, can we find him in our struggles to discern our purpose in life? Often we think we should be looking for a person, thing, or new circumstance and that this is where we should be focusing our efforts. But Jesus wants us to seek God first. Jesus is the tour guide of our lives; as Pope Francis says, he is "the faithful friend who never abandons us." Jesus is the one who can lead us to new doorways of existence. When we arrive at these doorways, we can knock. We have to act on these encounters with God—not necessarily pound on those doors, but we need to be courageously persistent in knocking until the door is opened. Like the widow in the aforementioned parable, we are not supposed to give up.

But I think one of the biggest problems preventing us from being granted what we ask for in our prayers is that we don't know what we want.

Now, I am a red-blooded American male. I love my wife and kids, football, and cold beer, and when conditions are just right (rude people, hot sauce, and lack of sleep), I can hurl curse words in the air that would make truck drivers and sailors high-five each other with delight. But there is something I have to confess. I really love *The Notebook*, the 2004 movie starring Ryan Gosling and Rachel McAdams. Intellectually, I know it's cheesy, and I realize that admitting my fondness for this movie means some people may tell me I have to surrender my Guy Card. In my defense, I contend that the film contains a scene that asks one of the most deeply spiritual questions that could ever be asked: "What do you want?"

In the movie, country boy Noah Calhoun (played by Gosling) has been smitten with rich girl Allie Hamilton (McAdams's character) ever since he first laid eyes on her when they were teenagers. They share a summer love affair and then go their separate ways, only to find that their hearts are still very much connected.

They meet again years later. Allie seems to have moved on; she's in love with someone else. But Noah? Well, Noah is still yearning for her. There is a confrontation that culminates with Noah repeatedly demanding of Allie, "WHAT DO YOU WANT? What do you want? What do you want? What-do-you-want?" Allie cannot answer his question. And so I ask you:

What do you want?

So many of us move through life as if we are in a fog, merely going through the motions, always feeling unsettled and uneasy, sensing that there is an unaddressed yearning inside us that never seems to go away. And yet few of us ever ask ourselves what is it that we really want. This is a question that can be difficult to answer, but once you do it in a sincere way, your life can be transformed.

In *The Jesuit Guide to (Almost) Everything*, James Martin covers this topic extraordinarily well. He recounts the Gospel story of blind Bartimaeus, who calls out to Jesus, only to be hushed by his friends. Jesus the acclaimed miracle worker is too busy to deal with the likes of you, Bartimaeus is told. But Jesus stops and asks Bartimaeus, "What do you want me to do for you?" The man replies, "Let me see again." Jesus answers, "Receive your sight. . . . Your faith has saved you."

Now, it's obvious to Jesus and to everyone else that this man is blind. Of course he wants to have his sight restored. And so we must pause and try to decipher why Jesus asks his petitioner what he wants. Martin writes: "Jesus asks Bartimaeus what he wants, not so much for himself as for the blind man. Jesus was helping the man identify his desire, and to be clear about it."

What we see in this story is that desire plus faith yields a miracle. I don't offer this equation as a magic formula. God is not a genie who grants wishes, and to think so is naive and misguided. But there is something interesting going on here. Bartimaeus is *sincere* in his request to be healed. So let's make a little adjustment: Desire plus *authentic* faith equals miracles. And by *authentic* I mean strong, true, and just.

Why is this process of identifying what we want so important? Let's allow Ron Rolheiser, author of *The Holy Longing* and *Sacred Fire*, to explain: "What lies deepest inside authentic faith is the truth that God is the object of all human desire, no matter how earthy and unholy that desire might seem at times. This implies that everything we desire is contained in God."

Yet, putting this into practice is a challenge. Rolheiser goes on to ask, "Do we really believe that God is the real object of our desires? When we look at all that is beautiful, full of life, attractive, sexually alluring, and pleasurable on earth, do we really think and believe that this is contained in an infinitely richer way inside of God and inside the life into which God invites us?" The answer for many of us is, quite simply, no.

But what if we tried a little experiment? What if we asked ourselves, "What do I want?" and just saw if we could trace the answer back to God?

Perhaps our seemingly superficial desire is to be able to acquire a new car. But—stick with me here—is this request only about transportation? Or maybe, just maybe, a new car would offer security. If you had a dependable vehicle, then you wouldn't have to worry about getting to work on time so that you can provide for your family. Well, God desires that you experience the joy of being a good provider for your family. If having a new car helps you fulfill this personal destiny, then maybe praying and working for a new car is not at odds with being in close communication with God. Let's consider another example. Perhaps your seemingly superficial desire to post everything about your life on Facebook or Instagram is actually more about your intense need to know that you matter, that someone cares for you, that you are not totally anonymous and irrelevant. Can you search that desire and then find peace in knowing that God is always there for you, that your presence here on earth is not accidental? That God had a plan in mind when he gave you life? Let's look at other desires that might at first glance seem to be disconnected from God. It could be you desire to travel or spend more time with your mother. Write this down. Then, take a good look at that desire and ask what is behind it. What is at the *heart* of this desire? (Remember, we're trying to get proficient at leading our heads back to our hearts.) And so figuring out what you really, *really* want should be an exercise that leads you straight to the heart of your yearnings. List whatever honest answers come to you. Don't be judgmental. Don't be superficial. Try this process for seven days, and while you're keeping this "desire journal," keep Noah Calhoun and his earnest question in mind. Noah *really* wants to know what Allie wants, but not exclusively for himself. He wants her to be clear about her decisions and the actions she takes based on those decisions. God wants exactly the same thing from us.

When we are clear about what we want, then we must formulate the request. Ask. Seek. Knock. Ask God for what you want in prayer, whether it is, for example, to be healed or for a loved one to be healed. Perhaps we are petitioning God for help getting back on track financially. If so, then we should make this petition part of a daily devotion. In other words, we should come to God with clearly formulated requests that reflect real-life needs. In the asking we learn a lot about ourselves and what we desire. And this should be done with enthusiasm. (I love that word, *enthusiasm!*) Enthusiasm comes from the Greek word *enthousiasmos*, "to be inspired," from the roots *en* and *theos*. To be enthusiastic is to have the Holy Spirit coursing through your whole being in a unique way. Ever meet someone who was truly enthusiastic? Someone who is moved by the Spirit? Ever seen Bruce Springsteen in concert? He's enthusiastic! He's got the fire, man! He's letting the Spirit do its thing through him. We all know how different life is when we live enthusiastically compared with living in a lukewarm state of being. There is an incalculable difference in the quality of life. And because God is generous about bestowing graces upon us, it seems to me that these graces should be accepted with enthusiasm! (Note my overuse of the exclamation point in this paragraph—it's all about my irrepressible enthusiasm!!)

Some years ago, a dear friend of mine told me her beloved grandmother had been diagnosed with cancer. She broke down crying. At some point I said, "I will pray for your grandmother. She's going to be all right." My friend, who had given up on God years ago after a series of disappointments and setbacks, gave me a sidelong glance that said, "Yeah, right. Like that will do any good."

Well, I went home and I prayed hard for my friend's grandmother, asking God to heal this woman I had never met. For two weeks I prayed night and day. During my lunch break I sought out quiet time at a local church, where I lit candles for my friend's grandmother. I even knocked on the door of a chapel one evening so I could be in a sacred place to pray. At a certain point I stopped praying, for no other reason than I got super busy at work and home. But my friend called me a couple of days later to say that something amazing had happened. Doctors had done tests on her grandmother before a scheduled operation and they didn't find a drop of cancer. They tested her twice and the results were the same. She was disease-free. My friend laughed and cried into the phone. "You were the only person that I know of who prayed for her. I think your prayers worked."

I have no idea if my prayers helped in this situation. Only God heals. I do know, though, that I prayed my heart out asking him for his help in the situation, and through it all I kept seeking him out in my requests. The best part of this story, though, is that my friend, who had given up on God, has now found him again.

So ask. But don't stop there. Push further by asking God what he needs from you. Often we focus only on our needs or the needs of others around us. Make asking God what his desires are a part of your devotional practice, and when you hear him knocking on your heart, let him in. Just let him in.

CHAPTER 9

Step 6: Cultivate Silence

For God alone, O my soul, wait in silence, for my hope is from him.

—PSALM 62:5

Prayer is not asking. Prayer is putting oneself in the hands of God, at His disposition, and listening to His voice in the depth of our hearts.

—MOTHER TERESA

Silence.

I am a husband and father. Like many such creatures, on Monday through Friday I commute to work on a crowded and often noisy train. On weekends you'll find me either spending time with my family or doing some sort of repair to our 1904 colonial house. Life means being busy doing all kinds of stuff, like just about everyone else I know (except Uncle Jerry . . . that guy doesn't do anything). There really isn't a lot of time to just be silent with God, which is precisely why I have a particular devotion to St. Ignatius.

Ignatius of Loyola, a soldier who lived in sixteenth-century Spain, found it hard to sit down, relax, and stay in one place quietly, even after part of his leg had been blown off in a battle. As a young man, he was a warrior who loved a good fight. There was another side to him, however, for he was also a romantic who had a penchant for the ladies and for reading tales of chivalry and adventure. But something happened to change his point of view. As he was recuperating from the injuries he had suffered during a skirmish with the French in Pamplona, Spain, in 1521, he began reading about Jesus and about the lives of the saints. This was not by choice. Actually, what was behind his reading spree was a desire to read the sixteenth-century version of *Fifty Shades of Grey* or *The Spaniard's Virgin Housekeeper* (seriously, that's a real book). He wanted to read about knights and fair maidens, but the home in which he was convalescing only had religious books on the bookshelves. Bored—but really, where could he go with a badly damaged leg?—he turned to the reading materials available just to pass the time. He soon discovered that reading about the lives of the saints was inspirational. Something stirred inside him. What that stirring indicated, he wasn't quite sure, but he began to comprehend that when he was thinking about God, he felt great. In contrast, when he thought about earthly things, he realized that his excitement for a beautiful woman and the prospect of going back into battle were, at best, fleeting, and the thought of either made him anxious. God equals feel good. Not God equals feel not so good. When he wasn't focused on heavenly matters, Ignatius felt like an outsider, and he didn't like it. He began spending more and more time with his focus on the Almighty; in time, he began a regular program of prayer that eventually led to the experience of divine visions. He began to see

God in all things, and this ability, this idea, would essentially become a driving force in his life. He became the founder of the Jesuit order and dedicated his life to Christ and to helping other like-minded men to seek God everywhere, in everything. Ignatius no longer felt lost; he found belonging in all of God's creation.

Silence is necessary for prayer, but it can also become a hindrance. Many people think that in order to pray they need to be alone or in a sanctuary, or their minds need to be utterly still and focused. Ignatius believed God always meets people where they are in their lives. You don't have to be a nun, a priest, or a monk to experience the divine. Busy mothers, fathers, and students can cultivate a God consciousness in actions they take every day. All of us can cultivate Ignatius's facility for seeing God in everything we do, from washing dishes to folding laundry, from commuting to work to writing research papers. When we look for God's presence in all of these things, we also find silence in all of these things. In fact, we can find time to pray everywhere—while standing in line at the DMV ("Thank you, God, for giving me the gift of my car and the ability to drive to work.") or while waiting for a prescription at a drugstore ("God, I'm so thankful that this medicine is going to help my child's infection. Please bless these antibiotics with a double dose of your healing power."). When we find God in everything, we become an embodiment of St. Paul's imperative to pray without ceasing. Why is unceasing prayer important? Precisely because it opens a constant direct line of communication with God that allows for the easy exchange of information, inspiration, and invigoration.

This heartfelt idea to cultivate silence in everything I do, to seize upon the quiet gaps between the things I do, the feelings I feel, and the thoughts I think, has been transformative in my spiritual life. Once I discovered the writings of St. Ignatius and began to embrace his ideas, I found that I was praying everywhere. I was praying while playing with my kids and while having dinner with my wife. I prayed on that crowded commuter train every day until the herd of sometimes-obnoxious people with whom I was moving no longer annoyed me. These people were transformed from faceless strangers into brothers and sisters (of course, it is true that brothers and sisters can get on our nerves, but you get what I mean).

This does not mean that we shouldn't go to church or seek sacred spaces where we can go to be alone with God and rest in awesome silence. But few of us feel as if we have the time to take this kind of break from what the world tells us we should be doing. It is easy to feel a sense of guilt when we try to escape, even for just a moment, from dealing with our worldly problems. Ignatius saw that addiction to busyness in himself, but he handled it by carving a bit of silence in everything he did. We can learn a great deal from his teachings. In fact, one of the best ways to benefit from Ignatius's experience is to use an exercise he popularized known as the Examen.

As mentioned earlier, mindfulness, the practice of mentally living in the present moment, has become quite popular in recent years. Dozens of books have been published about the subject. There are numerous apps available for download to help us become more focused. It is not difficult to find someone willing to teach us mindfulness either online, at a library, or at a local meditation or yoga center. While the practice is often associated with Eastern spirituality or yoga, Ignatius developed his own mindfulness technique. This is the Examen. Like a spiritual homing device, the Examen is a tool for bringing us closer to God.

Ignatius believed that it is often easy for us to overlook God in our actions and thoughts, just as the self-involved travelers passing the man in the ditch in the parable of the Good Samaritan. But, unlike with many contemporary mindfulness exercises, Ignatius believed it was important not only to pay attention to what was going on inside the head, but even more so to pay attention to what was going on inside the heart. While many think of the Examen as a mindfulness exercise, it can be seen even more crucially as a heartfulness exercise.

The Examen asks, first, what is drawing us near God and, second, what is drawing us away from God. What fears and worries are blocking us from seeing and feeling God in our lives? This practice is not meant to shame us if we feel we haven't lived up to either our expectations or his expectations. It's not meant to become an ego trip or a self-effacing put-down or a laundry list of wrongs we feel we've committed. Instead it's a method of realizing that our life matters and the things that we do or don't do have an impact on everyone around us. Think about it for just a moment: Everything we do has an effect on family, friends, strangers, the environment, the generations to come, and the world as a whole.

The Examen is usually performed at night before we go to sleep. It allows us to replay the day we are leaving behind and helps us become more aware of how to live out the next day. Here is what we do:

1) Ask God to Be Revealed

Imagine you're in a dark room with a dimmer switch. While some of us might feel as if we live in darkness all the time and can't see anything in front of us, many of us just feel like we're in a badly lit room. It's hard to make out what's in front of us, though we know something is there. It's definitely difficult to read the signs in front of us or to see the true color of the walls around us or of a painting in our midst. We ask God to increase the light in the room. When we pray for light, we don't ask to be blinded like Paul on the road to Damascus (though if that's what God wants for you, well, there isn't much you can do). Instead we can pray for a gradual change in our lives: "God, help me to see what's in the room with me. Help me to see the people and things in the world before me. Help me to see them better than I've seen them before. Help me to pay attention to the smiles or sadness on their faces and in their hearts. If it be your will, God, don't blind me. Just help me to see better."

2) Cultivate Gratitude

Give thanks for the day. Being thankful means giving thanks for all that we are and all that we have, even when we feel as if we have nothing. Giving thanks for the gift of life, the air we breathe, the water we drink, and the food we eat should become second nature. The clothes we wear and the homes that provide us shelter should be things about which we are prayerfully and thankfully aware. We might want more from life than what we are experiencing, but we can get that only when we truly become thankful for what we have right now. And so we must strive to become a spiritual private eye and search for clues to God's presence in all things. We must become proficient at giving thanks to God for co-workers who help us or courteous strangers who hold open doors. We should give thanks to God for the cell phone that allows us to stay in contact with our families and friends. We should focus on the people we meet during the day, everyone from the jovial security guard to the tired waitress in desperate need of sleep. We should pray for them, for strength, for happiness, for patience, and for love. We should give thanks to God for the person driving slowly in front of us when we're running late for a meeting or to pick up the kids from school. Maybe, just maybe, that laggard is God's way of slowing us down to protect us from being harmed in an accident.

3) Pay Attention to Your Emotions

As we've discussed earlier, sometimes our minds can get in the way of our hearts, but it's important to pay attention to our emotions. It's interesting to note that the word *emotion* has the word *motion* in it. Our emotions are the perceptions of experiences that *move* through us. They can stir things up, sometimes agitating us in both positive and negative ways, and they can muddy our lives. But they are supposed to move *through* us, to pass through our hearts so that we can move on with our lives. Too often, however, our minds create emotional stoppages. We suffer blocks when the emotions can't pass through us in a natural and safe manner. This is why part of the Examen is asking ourselves what kind of feelings we experienced during the day. Were we angry? Bored? Happy? Apathetic? Frightened? Were we able to let these emotions pass through us, or are we still holding on to them? We need to pay close attention to these experiences. We should be on the lookout for bottlenecked emotions. Ignatius believed that our emotions are able to carry us closer to God when they are free-flowing, just as they take us farther away from him when they result in barriers. What is God saying to you in the feelings you have about the day? What commentary might he be offering about life and the way you are living it?

It is good to pay attention to these emotional movements. If you are angry about something, the wise thing to do is to explore that anger. Perhaps someone said something to embarrass you at dinner. Maybe on another day you wouldn't have cared so much about what was said, but today you felt that the comment exposed a deeply held insecurity. The result is that you feel exposed and vulnerable, and that in turn makes you livid. These are all natural responses to stressful situations. What is God saying to you through it all? Often these are difficult questions to answer, so ask God to help you to understand your emotions and the feelings that come from them. Ask him for the grace to untangle these experiences, clear your emotional pathway, and allow the love in your heart to move into and out of you.

4) Choose Something Great That Happened Today and Pray About It

Here is an opportunity to become thankful, mindful, and heartful about one particular positive event in every day. Maybe you had a great conversation with a friend. Explore what made you feel good. Was it just laughs, or did you learn something? Pray for that friend; take that experience into your heart and ponder it there. Make the experience a prayer to God.

5) Ask, Where Was God for Me Today?

Was God walking with you? Was he present in your actions? Was he present in your feelings and thought? Ignatius asks us to seek God in all things, so the question becomes whether or not we see God in the less fortunate, or in people who are struggling in school, or in people going through a divorce. Did we treat all people fairly? If we didn't, then we know that we did not treat God fairly, either. If we are angry at our brother, we know that we are angry at God. We need to forgive, and if we are struggling to do so, then we need to ask God for the grace to forgive. Remember to bring it all back to ask, seek, knock. Ask God for the grace to forgive, seek and label the emotion that is inside, look for the strength and inspiration to do the right thing, and then knock on the door of your brother—either literally or by calling him on the phone, contacting him through e-mail or some other way, and then once you connect, reconcile. This doesn't mean that we allow people to use us as doormats or that we lower our standards and place ourselves in compromising positions. Rather, this means that we have been called to forgive others their trespasses.

6) Bless the Tomorrow

Ignatius advises us to ask God to continue to shine his light on us, helping us to see his presence in our lives. We should ask him to guide us on this journey we call life. Though this might seem almost rote or silly, asking God for directions is an important part of the spiritual journey. From time to time, all of us need to stop for directions. Ask God before you finish your Examen to point you toward the right way, and then ask again when you wake in the morning. Then let it be. Trust that God is guiding you in everything you are doing.

CHAPTER 10

Step 7: Give Your Life Away

Rejoice in hope, be patient in tribulation, be
constant in prayer.

—ROMANS 12:12

We're all kind of like quarterbacks. God snaps the ball of life to us. It becomes our job to pass that ball along to someone who can score. We're called to be like Jesus. He shares with people. He helps people. He gives thanks. Just like a quarterback, sometimes we stumble, sometimes we get sacked, and sometimes we throw an incomplete pass. But sometimes we help the "team"—that is to say, God's creation in all its wondrous forms—to reach the end zone. (There's a reason they call a long pass a Hail Mary!) Just give it away, man!

Jesus was a hero quarterback. He passed his life away to us. There is no greater gift. We're called to be like Jesus, to be heroic, even if we feel as frightened as Winnie the Pooh's friend Piglet. Heroism is about putting others first. You can be a heroic mom or dad, a heroic brother or sister, a heroic stranger. You can be heroic in your prayer life by putting God first and saying, "God, look, I talk all the time, but today I'm just going to listen. What can I do for you?" Put God first. Put Jesus first. Put the Holy Spirit first. And then we'll discover that we're putting the people around us first as well. All these firsts! They're the great paradox. Prayer helps get us to a place where we can live from a heroic heart. Sound daunting? Try it for a day and see what happens. David Bowie got it right: "We can be heroes, just for one day." Then try it again. I think in time it will become clear that we are leading a life of miracles each and every day.

Many of the devotions that follow in Part III of this book should take only a few minutes to do each day. I recommend that you try to set aside roughly fifteen minutes to cultivate a prayer life. That's just 1 percent of your life. The other 99 percent is all yours. But 1 percent of our day should be our starting place. The goal is to pray ceaselessly, love ceaselessly, and develop a perpetual relationship with God, his saints, and his angels so that we can get to know him better. We can move toward that attainment by making small changes in our daily lives. One of the things this book talks about, which I've been propounding for years, is how making small changes in the way we do things and being consistent in those actions can radically change our lives. For example, maybe prayer is tough for you. Start off by praying one minute a day. Do that for a week and then increase it by one minute every day for thirty days. At the end of that month you're giving 2 percent of your life to God in prayer. If you can pray fifteen minutes a day, at the end of the year you will have spent more than five thousand minutes in prayer. That's nearly four days of your life you've given to God! One of my favorite books is *The Practice of the Presence of God* by Brother Lawrence. In this short little volume, Brother Lawrence offers up everything he does as a prayer to God, which means that he is in a perpetual state of connection with the Almighty. Can we do that in the twenty-first century? I think we can. And we can start by dedicating just a few minutes to God every day.

The devotional life is one of perpetual intimacy, a life in which the heart does what the heart does: it connects us to God via love. Yes, people often associate the word *intimacy* only with something sexual. People get freaked out if you talk about intimacy between two people if they aren't in a committed relationship. But intimacy is really just about having a close friendship with another. And I think this modern sexual connotation keeps us from experiencing the great depths of friendship with others as well as with God. Heart speaks to heart; not everything has to do with sex. The enemy will try to make you think that way. But, as Freud said, sometimes a cigar is just a cigar. So to be intimate with God means to be in a deep friendship with him. We might forget that the Trinity is three persons, but if we develop friendships with those three very distinct persons, then we will be able to share our pains and struggles and joys more readily. Intimacy changes everything. It changes our perceptions, our awareness. When we move in this direction, we draw closer to union with God, to what T. S. Eliot calls the "still point of the turning world." It's then that we "arrive where we started and know the place for the first time."

SOME REMINDERS BEFORE PRAYING

To lead a devotional life is to surrender and humble ourselves before the Creator of all things. Always enter the sanctuary of your prayer life with an attitude of humility.

Take some time every day to pay attention to your thoughts and emotions. What are you thinking about before you enter into prayer? What are the feelings associated with these thoughts? Sometimes answers are readily available, but continue to ask the question. In time you'll begin to develop a balance between the head and the heart.

Make the sign of the cross. Bless yourself and your prayers. Be mindful and heartful. Pay attention to your thoughts and your emotions. Don't let past events block your head or your heart. Prayer is a time to share and let go. When there are no blockages, we have direct access and awareness of God.

Recite the Our Father. Remember the six points of the Lord's Prayer: praise God, be humble, ask God to meet your needs, live in a perpetual state of asking for forgiveness, don't be stupid and ask for or seek out temptation, and take evil seriously and pray for deliverance.

Ask, seek, knock. Be enthusiastic. Don't just pray once; pray all the time.

Cultivate silence. Try to make the Examen a daily part of life. Always be asking, "Where is God in this person? In this situation?"

Attempt to take your focus off yourself and place it on God.

Be consistent. It's very easy to forget to pray every day, and truth be told, our attention spans aren't what they might have been two decades ago. If praying a novena over nine consecutive days seems daunting, try praying one over three days during one week, three days the next, and three days the following. Set alarms or reminders on your cell phone to remind you to pray at certain times every day. Set a soft church bell ringtone to go off five minutes before you normally wake up, and spend that time in your devotion. Or set an alarm at three p.m. every day to draw your attention from all of your worldly activities to focus on God and be reminded that life everlasting is in the here and now.

Part III
The Devotions

All devotions, whether they honor the Virgin Mary, the saints, or the angels, should ultimately lead us to Christ, who then leads us to the Father. Jesus is the center of our lives, our beloved; his mother and his brothers and sisters in spirit are all part of a most holy family. Consider this for a moment: If you were deeply in love with someone, wouldn't you gain a unique understanding of that person by getting to know his or her family? This is what many Christian devotions aim to do; through prayer and meditation and developing a unique, ardent relationship with one of his family members, we can know our beloved better and better.

Let's begin with specific devotions in honor of the saints. I start with these prayers knowing that they are, by far, often the easiest entry points into the devotional life. I then present the angels, our heavenly aids throughout our day and when we're experiencing a crisis. We will then look at the Virgin Mary and some of the most powerful and beautiful of all devotions, and finally end with Jesus himself. All roads should lead to Jesus, and this book is no different.

In the pages that follow, I will offer simple introductions to these prayers and devotions, sometimes sharing personal stories to illuminate the traditional in the modern world. While the mechanics of these particular devotions often involve only a few words, they are some of the most powerful, penetrating, contemplative, miracle-working meditations that we can incorporate into our daily lives.

I have retained the traditional language in many of the prayers and devotions that we will encounter in the pages that follow, including the words thou, thee, thy, and thine. While many, like myself, have a penchant for these old-fashioned terms, there are some people who do not. Those readers should feel free to make the following substitutions if the Spirit moves them: for "thou" and "thee" use the word "you"; for "thy" use "your"; and for "thine" use "yours."

CHAPTER 11

Saints: Our Spiritual Lifesavers

Do not have any anxiety about the future. Leave everything
in God's hands for he will take care of you.

—ST. JOHN BAPTIST DE LA SALLE

What makes a saint? It is a question with many different answers, but here is one.

Many years ago, a psychotherapist asked a question: If you squeeze an orange, what comes out of it? The answer: orange juice. Why? Because that's what's in it. He then asked: What comes out of us when someone puts the squeeze on us? When you're under pressure? The answer is different for everyone, but I know personally my response would sometimes be fear, anger, outrage.

But here's a question the psychotherapist didn't ask: What came out of Jesus when the world put the squeeze on him? When he was abused, mocked, beaten, and crucified?

Courage, strength, love, and forgiveness. The world gave him pain and he gave back peace.

Jesus was the saintliest saint of all time. Hence, to be a saint—from the Latin word *sanctus*, meaning "holy"—is to live with the sacred spirit of Jesus in our hearts. To love courageously and unconditionally. To show mercy. To take the worst that the world offers and squeeze out peace and holiness.

This is not to say that the saints who tried to imitate Christ always acted holy. As author Thomas J. Craughwell has argued, many saints behaved, well, quite badly. St. Matthew was an extortionist. St. Augustine was a heretic and a playboy. St. Mary of Egypt was a seductress. St. Francis was a wastrel and St. Ignatius was an arrogant egotist. That is, until they turned their focus away from themselves and concentrated instead on Jesus.

God is love (1 John 4:8). If that's true, and if Christians believe that Jesus is God, then Jesus is love. So wherever we find Jesus's name in the Bible, we can substitute the word *love*.

The lives of the saints were lives of flawed human beings. But we know these individuals today precisely because they ultimately lived Jesus-centered, love-centered lives. Their careers represented dramatic U-turns that brought hope and healing to the suffering, education to the ignorant, and peace and solace to the tormented. In every other human being, they saw Jesus. They saw love. And they responded to interpersonal encounters with compassion, intelligence, and devotion. That's what you do when you meet love. You don't reject it. You embrace it.

Saints had their failings, quirks, and foibles; they were a mixture of virtue and vice. They made mistakes. They were tempted. And sometimes they were just downright not very nice. St. Paul talks about having a constant spiritual thorn in his side that often detracted him from focusing exclusively on God (it is somewhat indicative of his reputation that most people who met him hated him and wanted him dead). St. Teresa of Kolkata was known for being snippy and short-tempered. St. Jerome, who could often be mean-spirited, is considered one of the nastiest saints who ever lived. But when push came to shove, what came out of each one of them was, in a word, Jesus. Or in other words, God. Or in other words, love.

It is the saints' holiness and their humanness that make them great companions in our own efforts to develop a close relationship with Jesus. These very human men and women often feel more accessible in devotional practice than Jesus or the Virgin Mary might seem to be. It is easy to feel intimidated by Jesus's and Mary's awesome examples. It is as if their lights shine too brightly for our light-sensitive spiritual eyes. Those of us who have lived in caves of spiritual darkness sometimes need a little bit of time to adjust to their radiance. This is where a friend who's been there, done that, someone who is excited to be needed and helpful, someone who is patient and happy to help can act as a guide. These teachers can usher us into the warmth of the Son, which we want to feel on our own faces. They can be the sunglasses that help us trust enough to open wide our squinted eyes.

Though there are literally thousands of recognized saints in the Catholic Church, I'd like to highlight five who have had a unique influence in my life: St. Thérèse of Lisieux, St. Jude, St. Benedict, St. Francis, and St. Faustina.

ST. THÉRÈSE OF LISIEUX

Thérèse, a French Carmelite nun who lived in the last quarter of the nineteenth century, was an innocent soul who disliked posturing and pretentiousness. You could say she was in her spirit a Catholic Henry David Thoreau. Like the naturalist poet, Thérèse believed that we should simplify life down to its essence; less is more. She was intelligent but also sensitive and known for her emotional outbursts. She was shy and often bullied in school. But she was also spoiled, short of temper, and ambitious—not for material things but for spiritual experiences. Put plainly, it was Thérèse's ambition to become a saint.

Many saints are known for unusual accomplishments that involve miraculous healings for others. Thérèse has many devotees, some of whom came forward after her death with reports of miraculous intercession. One such person is the French singer Édith Piaf, who believes that the nun's supernatural intercession helped cure Édith of blindness when she was just a little girl.

Thérèse had a different concept of what it takes to be a saint. She reasoned that her path to sainthood would not lie in the performance of miracles, and so she did not focus on hugely flamboyant feats that were so spectacular they would capture the attention of the world. She never walked on water. She didn't go into the healing business. She didn't seek out lepers or poor people living on the periphery of society. Instead, Thérèse devoted her life to the minuscule. She lived a straightforward life that was obsessively focused on finding God in the small things that make up a day. She would make small sacrifices to God, such as sharing her dinner with someone else even though she was hungry. She found sublime worth in simple acts such as tending a garden, thereby helping to beautify her little corner of the world. She excelled in the performance of small deeds of kindness to everyone—family, convent sisters, and strangers alike. Thérèse was quite purposeful in her efforts to pave her road to the divine with small stones of mercy and compassion rather than with sturdy bricks of noticeable holiness. As she writes in her autobiography, *The Story of a*

Soul, "I will seek out a means of getting to Heaven by a little way—very short and very straight, a little way that is wholly new. We live in an age of inventions; nowadays the rich need not trouble to climb the stairs, they have lifts instead. Well, I mean to try and find a lift by which I may be raised unto God, for I am too tiny to climb the steep stairway of perfection. . . . Thine Arms, then, O Jesus, are the lift which must raise me up even unto Heaven. To get there I need not grow; on the contrary, I must remain little, I must become still less." Knowing that something as small as a seed can grow into a great tree, Thérèse spread and cultivated as many seeds of charity, compassion, and love as possible in hopes that God would notice and approve.

Thérèse's relentless appreciation of the everyday miracles that make up life is known as the Little Way.

I pray often with Thérèse. I ask for her intercession in my life. I seek her guidance in helping me to see the flowers she revered so greatly, she could not bring herself to pluck them from where they grew. I ask her to help me see beauty in the faces of the strangers I pass every day as I walk to work, and I ask for her help when I lose my humility and start becoming impatient on crowded trains. I cultivate an awareness of her Little Way as I am washing dishes or helping my son do his homework. And though I have a special devotion to Jesus and the Blessed Mother, I consider my devotion to the Little Flower as one of my most precious. Her Little Way helps to bring my heart closer to God in the experiences of the everyday. I don't need big miracles. St. Thérèse shows me that if I think about it, every little thing in life is nothing short of miraculous.

Prayer to St. Thérèse of Lisieux

St. Thérèse, flower of fervor and love, please intercede for us.
Fill our hearts with your pure love of God.
As we approach and celebrate your feast day, make us more
  aware of the goodness of God and how well he tends his
  garden. Instill in us your little way of doing ordinary
  things with extraordinary love.

Give us the heart of a child who wonders at life and
  embraces everything with loving enthusiasm. Teach us
  your delight in God's ways so that divine charity may
  blossom in our hearts.

Little Flower of Jesus, bring our petitions
(mention in silence here)
before God, our Father.

With your confidence, we come before Jesus as God's
  children, because you are our heavenly friend. As we
  celebrate the Feast Day of your homecoming in heaven,
  continue to shower roses and grace upon us.

Amen.

ST. JUDE

For most of my life I lived a few houses away from my grandmother. She was in many ways my second mom, and one of the
best friends I've ever had. As a boy, I would visit her almost every

day, sometimes for breakfast and sometimes for a snack of juice and pretzels after school. I would often do my homework at her house and I looked forward to hearing her stories about what it was like to grow up in Brooklyn during the 1930s. Once in a while she would punctuate her reminiscences and help me forget my troubles by dancing a bar or two of an Irish jig. My grandmother was gregarious. Irish to the core, she believed that a stranger was a friend she hadn't met yet. She talked to everyone—the people who worked at the local grocery, postal clerks, everyone. She was also a news junkie. When I came to her house after school, she would give me the rundown on all the major events going on around our town and across the world. By her example, I learned to pay attention, to be engaged in the world, to have equal passion for both the big picture and the little picture.

I continued making my pilgrimage to my grandmother's house as I grew older, throughout high school and college and even after I started my New York City career in publishing. One night after work, sometime around seven thirty, I was walking from the train station to my grandmother's house, wondering what news story she was going to share with me. As I crossed the street near her house, I heard her calling out to me, her voice screaming and hysterical. Alarmed, I ran to the old green-and-white house on Clinton, where my grandmother was leaning out the window, her face contorted in grief. "Grace has been calling you. Her father had a heart attack and died. Go to her, Gary. Go to her!"

"What? *No!*"

I reached into my pocket and pulled out my cell phone. Earlier in the day during a work meeting I had turned it to silent mode and had forgotten to switch it back on. There were ten messages flashing on the screen.

I raced to my car, which was parked down the block not far from my grandmother's house, and as I ran I could hear my grandmother telling me, "Pray for her! Pray for her!"

I drove like a maniac toward Grace's home one town away. I blew right through traffic lights. I took a shortcut on the road that curved through Hempstead Lake State Park. I flipped open my phone and started listening to the messages. Grace was crying. Her father had felt ill. Her mom and brother took him to the hospital. Grace stayed behind to make soup for when he got home, but he had died in the hospital.

In this moment I recalled that Grace's father's favorite saint was Jude. I turned to St. Jude, the patron saint of lost causes, for help. "St. Jude, please make this all a big mistake. Please make this all a big mistake. Please save him. Please, St. Jude. Help."

When I arrived at Grace's house, I was still holding out hope that this was all some kind of a mistake, that her father was in the hospital, recovering but alive. But then Grace opened the door. I stepped into the living room and saw everyone in her immediate family in tableau, mute with shock and grief. In a split second it became obvious that my prayer to St. Jude had not been answered.

Jude, also known as Thaddeus, was one of the twelve original apostles. He doesn't get much face time in the New Testament (he asks Jesus a question in the Gospel of John: "Lord, how is it that you will reveal yourself to us, and not to the world?" and there is a letter attributed to him known as the Epistle of Jude); nonetheless, he has become the patron saint of desperate situations. Jude is often depicted with a flame, signifying the sacred fire of the Holy Spirit, over his head. He carries an image of Jesus over his heart, and in his left hand he carries a staff as a symbol of his martyrdom.

This, however, was way beyond a hopeless cause. In fact, that night was horrific. Grace's family and I were experiencing what Elisabeth Kübler-Ross identified as the first stage of grief: denial. How could something like this happen? How could God let this happen? Why wasn't St. Jude there to protect Grace's father and help him get to the hospital in time to be saved?

Of course, I have no answers to those questions. But in the days, weeks, and months that followed, St. Jude seemed to be close at hand, watching over Grace's family, offering all of us consolation and strength just exactly when we were at our lowest. One possible manifestation in particular that seemed to be divinely inspired happened on the day of the funeral. The family had been sitting around the dinner table, talking about the church service earlier in the day. At one point the conversation turned to St. Jude. Grace's father's beeper—more common than cell phones in 1997—went off. Grace's brother checked the beeper to see who was calling, and the number on the device indicated that the call was coming from their house. Eerily, no one sitting around the table was near a phone. To this day none of us know exactly what happened at that moment, but our faith tells us that Grace's father and St. Jude were phoning as if to say, "All is well; I am with you always."

Prayer to St. Jude

Most holy apostle, St. Jude, faithful servant and friend of Jesus, the Church honors and invokes you universally as the patron of hope. Please intercede on my behalf. Make use of that particular privilege given to you to bring hope, comfort, and help where they are needed most. Come to my assistance in this great need that I may receive the consolation and help of heaven as I work with my challenges, particularly [here, make your request]. I praise God with you and all the saints forever. I promise, blessed St. Jude, to be ever mindful of this great favor, to always honor you as my special and powerful patron, and to gratefully encourage devotion to you. Amen.

ST. BENEDICT

Some years ago, while doing research for a book I was writing about the supernatural, a friend of mine, a Catholic deacon, asked if I would attend a prayer service for a woman who was purportedly possessed by demons. Feeling in equal parts honored, frightened, intimidated, and intrigued, I told him I would think about it.

I had read that exorcisms and demonic cleansing ceremonies had been on the rise in the early years of the twenty-first century, particularly in Italy, where more than four hundred thousand exorcisms were requested each year. Even so, I was surprised to learn that they were happening essentially in our own backyards here in the States. As you can tell, I'm a firm believer in the unseen world of invisible realities (God, Jesus, the Holy Spirit, the Virgin Mary, angels, and saints), but I had not yet articulated a personal philosophy of demons and the devil. To be honest, I preferred not to think about that sort of thing. Weren't people who claimed to be possessed by the devil just those with psychiatric disorders, perhaps trying to disassociate from their own feelings and actions? Still, I was curious, so after having deliberated over the consequences of accepting the invitation, I told my friend that I would indeed attend the service and would help in any way I could.

One week later I found myself in the basement of a church in New York. It was a steamy summer evening and there was no air-conditioning in this utilitarian room filled with folding chairs. A couple of box fans scattered at random whirred noisily. The room was packed with at least two hundred people who had come to participate in a Latino prayer service. Though I didn't speak Spanish well, I had been serving as a prayer minister to the deacon for the past few months, which meant that I would assist him during the blessings he performed at the end of services such as these. This meant the laying on of hands, usually on someone's head or shoulders, and the praying of prayers in which the deacon and I would call upon Jesus and the Holy Spirit to heal whatever personal ailments or family problems might be troubling the petitioner standing in front of us. I felt keenly honored to have been asked to be part of this ministry, especially since I had grown up in a church community where hardly anyone sang and people rarely smiled during worship services, and some even turned away when we were supposed to shake hands at the end of Mass. For me, then, these hands-on prayer services were intimate in a way that was new to me. They were emotionally and spiritually inspirational, with joyous singing and enthusiastic responses coming from those in attendance. Though I understood precious few words, the fervor and dedication of the attendees at these Spanish-language services made me feel as if I had found a spiritual home.

At the end of this particular service, after most of the people had left, the woman supposedly possessed by demons was brought out to the center of the room. I told my deacon friend that I was going to pray from a short distance—partly out of fear and partly because I wanted to be an observer. I added that if he really needed me, he could just give me a look and I would be by his side in a flash.

I pulled my St. Benedict medal, known to protect a person from demonic entities, from my pocket and held it in my hand. I leaned against a wall with another friend of mine. The two of us watched as the deacon and a small group of ministers began praying over the woman, who was seated in a chair. Their voices droned softly, just a low murmur escaping from bowed heads. For the first few minutes nothing seemed to be happening. Then, the woman began exhibiting signs of agitation. The deacon's voice rose. I heard him call out, "Ven, espíritu santo" (Come, Holy Spirit), as he sprinkled the woman with holy water. I heard a terrifying, guttural sound rise up from within the circle. Two of the woman's family members forcibly held her down in the chair as her face contorted and her body writhed. She started speaking so quickly and aggressively, I couldn't make out whether she was speaking Spanish or some other strange tongue.

My friend and I, backs to the wall, added our prayers to those being said for this woman. I pressed my thumb against what many call the devil-chasing medal and repeated the Lord's Prayer in English. The energy in the room seemed to electrify and an already stifling room became hotter and hotter.

At a certain point the deacon placed his hands on the woman's head and, praying, cried out in such a loud voice that everyone in the room was startled. I assumed that he was trying to silence whatever might be inside her, whether that being was a dark spirit or the woman's own neurosis. Her body went stiff and seemed to lift off the ground, and her mouth opened wide. For a moment there was no sound, and then I heard a scream like the roar of a ferocious animal. The woman collapsed into the arms of her family and fell silent.

Now, I was unsure of what I thought I saw next, but as the room began to return to some semblance of normalcy, I saw a faint but dark cloud slither along the floor right in front of me and then disappear under a door.

I turned to my friend. He turned to me.

"Did you see that?" I asked.

"I saw something."

"What was it?"

"I have no idea."

To this day we still don't. What we saw could have been a shadow cast by someone moving in the room, though we both agree that there didn't seem to be any movement coming from the prayer circle.

Maybe it was a visual anomaly. It was, after all, rather hot in the basement.

Or maybe it was something else.

I put my St. Benedict medal back in my pocket. I made the sign of the cross and walked over to see how the woman and the deacon were doing. They seemed to be fine. And then I went home.

Was there a demonic entity in that woman? Did the deacon exorcise a dark spirit that night? Or was the woman just suffering from emotional or psychological issues? Did my prayers help at all? There's no way of knowing, although I know, through follow-up, that this woman is living what seems to be a happy and contented life today.

For centuries, the St. Benedict medal, like the one I had that night, has been used to ward off evil and protect believers from the wickedness and snares of the devil. The object itself isn't a talisman; this detailed piece of metal has no power in and of itself. Any authority comes from a combination of God's influence and the expression of our faith. Many who believe in the evil eye or the ability of someone to intentionally or unintentionally curse another through envy and negative intentions carry the medal with them as a reminder that God's goodness is stronger than anything else in our world. Though the true history of this object has been obscured over time, a devotion to St. Benedict is often credited with helping a young, pious boy survive a deadly snakebite in the eleventh century. That youth would grow up to become Pope Leo IX, who urged Catholics to cultivate a special relationship with the man who developed the Benedictine monastic rule (a set of principles for living a Godly life) and to rely on the medal in times of need.

Like the Miraculous Medal, St. Benedict's emblem is rich in imagery and symbolism. On the front of the mysterious medal is an image of St. Benedict with light radiating outward from his head. In his left hand he holds a book symbolizing his rules for living; in his right he holds a cross. An eagle and a chalice sit on an altar. Inscribed in almost microscopic letters near Benedict's arms are the words *Crux sancti patris Benedicti* (The cross of our holy father Benedict). Around the perimeter of the medal are the words *Eius in obitu nostro praesentia muniamur* (May his presence protect us in our deaths). Beneath Benedict's feet is written "1880," the year the current version of the medal was created. The cross of St. Benedict is featured on the back of the medal, crowned by the word *Pax* (Peace). Around the edge is a series of letters: *VRS-NSMV-SMQL-IVB.* Each set of letters is an abbreviated form of a Latin invocation:

VRS—Vade retro Satana—Step back, Satan

NSMV—Nunquam suade mihi vana—Do not tempt me with your vanity

SMQL—Sunt mala quae libas—What you offer is evil

IVB—Ipse venena bibas—Drink your own poison

On the bars of the cross are the letters *CSSML*, the Latin abbreviation of *Crux sacra sit mihi lux* (The holy cross is my light) and *NDSMD, Nunquam draco sit mihi dux* (Never let the dragon guide me). The four letters around the arms of the cross repeat what is imprinted on the front: *Crux sancti patris Benedicti* (The cross of our holy father Benedict).

That's a lot of coding for such a small piece of metal. All the Latin abbreviations make it seem like an element from a Dan Brown novel. But millions have used the medal to protect themselves from evil. Many building contractors will bury the medals in the foundations of new structures to protect their inhabitants from misfortune. Many have used the medal to help overcome addiction and alcoholism.

Prayer to St. Benedict

Dear St. Benedict, I thank God for showering you with his grace to love him above all else and to establish a monastic rule that has helped so many of his children live full and holy lives.

Through the cross of Jesus Christ, I ask you to please intercede that God might protect me, my loved ones, my home, property, possessions, and workplace today and always by your holy blessing, that we may never be separated from Jesus, Mary, and the company of all the blessed. Through your intercession may we be delivered from temptation, spiritual oppression, physical ills, and disease. Protect us from drug and alcohol abuse, impurity and immorality, objectionable companions, and negative attitudes.

In Jesus's name, amen.

Novena to St. Benedict (to Be Recited over Nine Days)

Glorious St. Benedict, sublime model of virtue, pure vessel of God's grace! Behold me humbly kneeling at your feet. I implore you in your loving kindness to pray for me before the throne of God. To you I have recourse in the dangers that daily surround me. Shield me against my selfishness and my indifference to God and to my neighbor. Inspire me to imitate you in all things. May your blessing be with me always, so that I may see and serve Christ in others and work for his kingdom.

Graciously obtain for me from God those favors and graces which I need so much in the trials, miseries, and afflictions of life. Your heart was always full of love, compassion, and mercy toward those who were afflicted or troubled in any way. You never dismissed without consolation and assistance anyone who had recourse to you. I therefore invoke your powerful intercession, confident in the hope that you will hear my prayer and obtain for me the special grace and favor I earnestly implore: [name it].

Help me, great St. Benedict, to live and die as a faithful child of God, to run in the sweetness of his loving will and to attain the eternal happiness of heaven. Amen.

ST. FRANCIS

On July 11, 1986, New York City police detective Steve McDonald and his partner, Sergeant Peter King, stopped three teenagers acting suspiciously in Central Park to question them about a series of recent bicycle thefts. As author Johann Christoph Arnold chronicles in his book *Why Forgive?*, McDonald approached one of the boys, who seemed to be carrying a gun. Another member of the group, fifteen-year-old Shavod Jones, fired three shots at the officer; bullets hit him in his head, throat, and back. McDonald, newly married with a child on the way, was twenty-nine years old at the time. The last bullet shattered his spinal cord.

The young men scattered as the detective crumpled to the ground. King radioed in a police code for officer in need of assistance. When first responders arrived, they saw King holding McDonald in his arms, the two of them covered in blood.

With injuries so ghastly they seemed beyond life-threatening, it was a miracle that McDonald survived. However, the damage to his body rendered him paralyzed from the neck down. McDonald would never fully recover from the injuries. For the rest of his life, he would be confined to a wheelchair and bound to a respirator. He would never play football with his son, Conor, born six months after the attack. Never would he be able to walk with his family through beautiful Central Park in the summer.

Shavod Jones was captured and sentenced to prison. Most of us would have wanted our assailant to rot in jail (and maybe even rot in hell). But McDonald wasn't like most of us. Journalist Michael Daly noted in the *Daily Beast* that while the detective was confined to the hospital during the days following the shooting, he met Mychal Judge. This friar and Catholic priest, who would later die ministering to the injured and dead in the North Tower of the World Trade Center on September 11, 2001, introduced McDonald to a prayer that would change the cop's life forever after:

> *Lord, make me an instrument of your peace:*
> *where there is hatred, let me sow love;*
> *where there is injury, pardon;*
> *where there is doubt, faith;*
> *where there is despair, hope;*
> *where there is darkness, light;*
> *where there is sadness, joy.*

This prayer, attributed to St. Francis, a medieval monk known for his love of nature, animals, and the poor, would become a sacred devotion for McDonald and his family. These words gave him strength. The prayer gave him purpose. It allowed love to enter his broken body and heal his wounded heart.

Privately and publicly, McDonald forgave Jones and even tried to start a friendship with the teen by corresponding with him through a series of letters. As McDonald himself recounted in Arnold's book:

> I was a badge to that kid, a uniform representing the government. I was the system that let landlords charge rent for squalid apartments in broken-down tenements; I was the city agency that fixed up poor neighborhoods and drove the residents out, through gentrification.... To Shavod Jones, I was the enemy. He didn't see me as a per-

son, as a man with loved ones, as a husband and father-to-be. He'd bought into all the stereotypes of his community: the police are racist, they'll turn violent, so arm yourself against them. And I couldn't blame him. Society—his family, the social agencies responsible for him . . . had failed him way before he had met me in Central Park.

Though they kept in touch over the years, McDonald and his attacker would never again meet face-to-face. Three days after Jones was released on parole in September 1995, the young man, just twenty-five at the time, died from head injuries sustained in a motorcycle accident while popping wheelies with a friend in East Harlem.

A few years ago, I became a lector at St. Agnes Cathedral on Long Island and would often see McDonald with his wife, Patti Ann, at Sunday church services. There in the front row, he sat in his wheelchair, connected to the breathing tube that kept him alive, eyes bright and sharp. In his eyes I saw a focus on the invisible reality that is all around us: God. In McDonald, I saw a man who, like Francis of Assisi, embodied Jesus.

Forgive. And love.

McDonald is probably the closest I'll ever come to being in the presence of a living saint. Still, how was he able to absolve someone who had sentenced him to a life as a quadriplegic? McDonald provides an answer in Arnold's book:

> I forgave Shavod because I believe the only thing worse than receiving a bullet in my spine would have been to nurture revenge in my heart. Such an attitude would have extended my injury to my soul, hurting my wife, son, and

others even more. It's bad enough that the physical effects are permanent, but at least I can choose to prevent spiritual injury. . . . I have my ups and downs. Some days, when I am not feeling very well, I can get angry. I get depressed. There have been times when I even felt like killing myself. But I have come to realize that anger is a wasted emotion. . . . Of course, I didn't forgive Shavod right away. It took time. . . . But I can say this: I've never regretted forgiving him.

Forgiveness can be very difficult for many of us. We can hold on to past hurts the way the body can hold on to cholesterol and fat, causing it to form plaque that builds up and hardens in our arteries. Anger and resentment are the saturated and trans fats of the spiritual life; they lead to the narrowing of our hearts, which ultimately can cause our souls to darken with disease. Yet, McDonald, though his body was ravaged, was the archetype of spiritual health, a modern-day example of forgiveness in action.

McDonald's body finally gave out on January 10, 2017, nearly thirty years after the shooting. He was fifty-nine years old. At his funeral, his son Conor, now a sergeant for the New York City Police Department, read his father's favorite prayer to a hushed congregation. It was a prayer McDonald lived in his heart. It would do the whole world a lot of good if we lived it in our own hearts as well.

Prayer of St. Francis

Lord, make me an instrument of your peace:
where there is hatred, let me sow love;
where there is injury, pardon;
where there is doubt, faith;
where there is despair, hope;
where there is darkness, light;
where there is sadness, joy.
O divine Master, grant that I may not so much seek
to be consoled as to console,
to be understood as to understand,
to be loved as to love.
For it is in giving that we receive,
it is in pardoning that we are pardoned,
and it is in dying that we are born to eternal life.
Amen.

ST. FAUSTINA AND
THE DIVINE MERCY OF JESUS

I was first introduced to the Divine Mercy while enrolled in pastoral formation in 2007. At the time I was considering studying to become a deacon of the Catholic Church, but after much discernment I decided that I needed to spend my time with my wife and young sons instead of serving the bishop of our diocese. While I took a great deal away from those theology classes and training, it is this particular devotion that has had the greatest impact on my life.

The Divine Mercy of Jesus was revealed to a young, uneducated Polish nun named Faustina Kowalska through a series of apparitions she experienced in the years before World War II. In these mystical encounters, Jesus requested that a painting of himself be crafted with the words *Jesus, I Trust in Thee*. In the image (as depicted in the frontispiece at the beginning of this book), beams of red and white light emanate from the heart of Jesus, the colors symbolizing the merciful blood and water that poured from his body at his crucifixion. It was that sacrifice and the love behind it that radically changed the course of human history. Those who meditate and pray with the image of Divine Mercy are reminded that God wants us to ask him to let his mercy pour out on all the world, that we should be merciful to others, and that the more we trust in Jesus, the more we'll receive grace and blessings in our lives. As St. Faustina writes in her spiritual journals, which have come to be known as *Diary: Divine Mercy in My Soul*, "When I see that the burden is beyond my strength, I do not consider or analyze it or probe into it, but I run like a child to the Heart of Jesus and say only one word to Him: 'You can do all things.' And then I keep silent, because I know that Jesus Himself will intervene in the matter, and as for me, instead of tormenting myself, I use that time to love Him."

What follows is the Divine Mercy chaplet and a novena that will draw you closer to Jesus and allow his mercy to be poured out on you.

The Chaplet of the Divine Mercy is recited using five decades of rosary beads as a way to meditate on God's loving mercy and compassion. It is normally prayed at three p.m. every day as a reminder that Jesus died at three p.m. on Good Friday. I have an alarm set on my phone for just that time to remind me of the Divine Mercy that is at the center of our devotional life.

The Divine Mercy Chaplet

1. Make the sign of the cross

2. Optional opening prayers
   You expired, Jesus, but the source of life gushed forth for souls, and the ocean of mercy opened up for the whole world. O Fount of Life, unfathomable Divine Mercy, envelop the whole world and empty yourself out upon us. *(Repeat three times.)*
   O Blood and Water, which gushed forth from the heart of Jesus as a fountain of mercy for us, I trust in you!

3. Our Father
   Our Father, who art in heaven, hallowed be thy name; thy kingdom come; thy will be done on earth as it is in heaven. Give us this day our daily bread; and forgive us our trespasses as we forgive those who trespass against us; and lead us not into temptation, but deliver us from evil. Amen.

4. Hail Mary
   Hail Mary, full of grace. The Lord is with thee. Blessed art thou amongst women, and blessed is the fruit of thy womb, Jesus. Holy Mary, Mother of God, pray for us sinners, now and at the hour of our death. Amen.

5. The Apostles' Creed
   I believe in God, the Father almighty, Creator of heaven

and earth, and in Jesus Christ, his only son, our Lord, who was conceived by the Holy Spirit, born of the Virgin Mary, suffered under Pontius Pilate, was crucified, died, and was buried; he descended into hell; on the third day he rose again from the dead; he ascended into heaven, and is seated at the right hand of God the Father almighty; from there he will come to judge the living and the dead. I believe in the Holy Spirit, the holy Catholic Church, the communion of saints, the forgiveness of sins, the resurrection of the body, and life everlasting. Amen.

6. The Eternal Father
   Eternal Father, I offer you the Body and Blood, Soul and Divinity of your dearly beloved son, Our Lord, Jesus Christ, in atonement for our sins and those of the whole world.

7. On the ten small beads of each decade
   For the sake of his sorrowful Passion, have mercy on us and on the whole world.

8. Repeat for the remaining decades
   Say the Eternal Father on the Our Father bead and then say ten "For the sake of his sorrowful Passion" prayers on the following Hail Mary beads.

9. Conclude with Holy God (repeat three times)
   Holy God, Holy Mighty One, Holy Immortal One, have mercy on us and on the whole world.

10. Optional closing prayer

     Eternal God, in whom mercy is endless and the treasury
     of compassion, inexhaustible, look kindly upon us and
     increase your mercy in us, that in difficult moments we
     might not despair nor become despondent, but with
     great confidence submit ourselves to your holy will,
     which is love and mercy itself.

Novena to the Divine Mercy of Jesus
(to Be Recited over Nine Days)

Jesus instructed Sister Faustina to write down this novena during
one of her visions. Although it is recited beginning on Good Friday, many people pray this novena throughout the year when they
need to draw closer to God's heart. Each day of the novena begins
with Jesus speaking directly to us.

First Day

     Today bring to Me all mankind, especially all sinners,
     and immerse them in the ocean of My mercy. In this
     way you will console Me in the bitter grief into which
     the loss of souls plunges Me.

     Most Merciful Jesus, whose very nature it is to have
     compassion on us and to forgive us, do not look upon
     our sins but upon our trust which we place in Your
     infinite goodness. Receive us all into the abode of Your
     Most Compassionate Heart, and never let us escape
     from It. We beg this of You by Your love which unites
     You to the Father and the Holy Spirit.

     Eternal Father, turn Your merciful gaze upon all

mankind and especially upon poor sinners, all enfolded in the Most Compassionate Heart of Jesus. For the sake of His sorrowful Passion show us Your mercy, that we may praise the omnipotence of Your mercy for ever and ever. Amen.

Second Day

Today bring to Me the Souls of Priests and Religious, and immerse them in My unfathomable mercy. It was they who gave me strength to endure My bitter Passion. Through them as through channels My mercy flows out upon mankind.

Most Merciful Jesus, from whom comes all that is good, increase Your grace in men and women consecrated to Your service, that they may perform worthy works of mercy; and that all who see them may glorify the Father of Mercy who is in heaven.

Eternal Father, turn Your merciful gaze upon the company of chosen ones in Your vineyard—upon the souls of priests and religious; and endow them with the strength of Your blessing. For the love of the Heart of Your Son in which they are enfolded, impart to them Your power and light, that they may be able to guide others in the way of salvation and with one voice sing praise to Your boundless mercy for ages without end. Amen.

Third Day

Today bring to Me all Devout and Faithful Souls, and immerse them in the ocean of My mercy. These souls brought me consolation on the Way of the Cross. They were a drop of consolation in the midst of an ocean of bitterness.

Most Merciful Jesus, from the treasury of Your mercy, You impart Your graces in great abundance to each and all. Receive us into the abode of Your Most Compassionate Heart and never let us escape from It. We beg this grace of You by that most wondrous love for the heavenly Father with which Your Heart burns so fiercely.

Eternal Father, turn Your merciful gaze upon faithful souls, as upon the inheritance of Your Son. For the sake of His sorrowful Passion, grant them Your blessing and surround them with Your constant protection. Thus may they never fail in love or lose the treasure of the holy faith, but rather, with all the hosts of Angels and Saints, may they glorify Your boundless mercy for endless ages. Amen.

Fourth Day

Today bring to Me those who do not believe in God and those who do not know Me, I was thinking also of them during My bitter Passion, and their future zeal comforted My Heart. Immerse them in the ocean of My mercy.

Most compassionate Jesus, You are the Light of the whole world. Receive into the abode of Your Most Compassionate Heart the souls of those who do not believe in God and of those who as yet do not know You. Let the rays of Your grace enlighten them that they, too, together with us, may extol Your wonderful mercy; and do not let them escape from the abode which is Your Most Compassionate Heart.

Eternal Father, turn Your merciful gaze upon the souls of those who do not believe in You, and of those who as yet do not know You, but who are enclosed in the Most Compassionate Heart of Jesus. Draw them to the light of the Gospel. These souls do not know what great happiness it is to love You. Grant that they, too, may extol the generosity of Your mercy for endless ages. Amen.

Fifth Day

Today bring to Me the Souls of those who have separated themselves from My Church, and immerse them in the ocean of My mercy. During My bitter Passion they tore at My Body and Heart, that is, My Church. As they return to unity with the Church, My wounds heal and in this way they alleviate My Passion.

Most Merciful Jesus, Goodness Itself, You do not refuse light to those who seek it of You. Receive into the abode of Your Most Compassionate Heart the souls of those who have separated themselves from Your Church. Draw them by Your light into the unity of the Church, and do not let them escape from the abode of Your Most Compassionate Heart; but bring it about that they, too, come to glorify the generosity of Your mercy.

Eternal Father, turn Your merciful gaze upon the souls of those who have separated themselves from Your Son's Church, who have squandered Your blessings and misused Your graces by obstinately persisting in their errors. Do not look upon their errors, but upon the love of Your own Son and upon His bitter Passion, which He underwent for their sake, since they, too, are enclosed in His Most Compassionate Heart. Bring it about that they also may glorify Your great mercy for endless ages. Amen.

Sixth Day

Today bring to Me the Meek and Humble Souls and the Souls of Little Children, and immerse them in My mercy. These souls most closely resemble My Heart. They strengthened Me during My bitter agony. I saw them as earthly Angels, who will keep vigil at My altars. I pour out upon them whole torrents of grace. I favor humble souls with My confidence.

Most Merciful Jesus, You yourself have said, "Learn from Me for I am meek and humble of heart." Receive into the abode of Your Most Compassionate Heart all meek and humble souls and the souls of little children. These souls send all heaven into ecstasy and they are the heavenly Father's favorites. They are a sweet-smelling bouquet before the throne of God; God Himself takes delight in their fragrance. These souls have a permanent abode in Your Most Compassionate Heart, O Jesus, and they unceasingly sing out a hymn of love and mercy.

Eternal Father, turn Your merciful gaze upon meek souls, upon humble souls, and upon little children who are enfolded in the abode which is the Most

Compassionate Heart of Jesus. These souls bear the closest resemblance to Your Son. Their fragrance rises from the earth and reaches Your very throne. Father of mercy and of all goodness, I beg You by the love You bear these souls and by the delight You take in them: Bless the whole world, that all souls together may sing out the praises of Your mercy for endless ages. Amen.

Seventh Day

Today bring to Me the Souls who especially venerate and glorify My Mercy, and immerse them in My mercy. These souls sorrowed most over my Passion and entered most deeply into My spirit. They are living images of My Compassionate Heart. These souls will shine with a special brightness in the next life. Not one of them will go into the fire of hell. I shall particularly defend each one of them at the hour of death.

Most Merciful Jesus, whose Heart is Love Itself, receive into the abode of Your Most Compassionate Heart the souls of those who particularly extol and venerate the greatness of Your mercy. These souls are mighty with the very power of God Himself. In the midst of all afflictions and adversities they go forward, confident of Your mercy; and united to You, O Jesus, they carry all mankind on their shoulders. These souls will not be judged severely, but Your mercy will embrace them as they depart from this life.

Eternal Father, turn Your merciful gaze upon the souls who glorify and venerate Your greatest attribute, that of Your fathomless mercy, and who are enclosed in the Most Compassionate Heart of Jesus. These souls are a living Gospel; their hands are full of deeds of mercy, and their hearts, overflowing with joy, sing a canticle of mercy to You, O Most High! I beg You O God:

Show them Your mercy according to the hope and trust they have placed in You. Let there be accomplished in them the promise of Jesus, who said to them that during their life, but especially at the hour of death, the souls who will venerate this fathomless mercy of His, He, Himself, will defend as His glory. Amen.

Eighth Day

Today bring to Me the Souls who are in the prison of Purgatory, and immerse them in the abyss of My mercy. Let the torrents of My Blood cool down their scorching flames. All these souls are greatly loved by Me. They are making retribution to My justice. It is in your power to bring them relief. Draw all the indulgences from the treasury of My Church and offer them on their behalf. Oh, if you only knew the torments they suffer, you would continually offer for them the alms of the spirit and pay off their debt to My justice.

Most Merciful Jesus, You Yourself have said that You desire mercy; so I bring into the abode of Your Most Compassionate Heart the souls in Purgatory, souls who are very dear to You, and yet, who must make retribution to Your justice. May the streams of Blood and Water which gushed forth from Your Heart put out the flames of Purgatory, that there, too, the power of Your mercy may be celebrated.

Eternal Father, turn Your merciful gaze upon the souls suffering in Purgatory, who are enfolded in the Most Compassionate Heart of Jesus. I beg You, by the sorrowful Passion of Jesus Your Son, and by all the bitterness with which His most sacred Soul was flooded: Manifest Your mercy to the souls who are under Your just scrutiny. Look upon them in no other way but only through the Wounds of Jesus, Your dearly beloved Son; for we firmly believe that there is no limit to Your goodness and compassion. Amen.

Ninth Day

Today bring to Me the Souls who have become Lukewarm, and immerse them in the abyss of My mercy. These souls wound My Heart most painfully. My soul suffered the most dreadful loathing in the Garden of Olives because of lukewarm souls. They were the reason I cried out: "Father, take this cup away from Me, if it be Your will." For them, the last hope of salvation is to run to My mercy.

Most compassionate Jesus, You are Compassion Itself. I bring lukewarm souls into the abode of Your Most Compassionate Heart. In this fire of Your pure love, let these tepid souls who, like corpses, filled You with such deep loathing, be once again set aflame. O Most Compassionate Jesus, exercise the omnipotence of Your mercy and draw them into the very ardor of Your love, and bestow upon them the gift of holy love, for nothing is beyond Your power.

Eternal Father, turn Your merciful gaze upon

lukewarm souls who are nonetheless enfolded in the Most Compassionate Heart of Jesus. Father of Mercy, I beg You by the bitter Passion of Your Son and by His three-hour agony on the Cross: Let them, too, glorify the abyss of Your mercy. Amen.

CHAPTER 12

Angels: Our Constant Guardians

You never know what worse luck your bad luck
has saved you from.

—CORMAC MCCARTHY

In the *Duino Elegies*, a series of ten poems about life, death, and the angels who move between their world and ours, the poet Rainer Maria Rilke famously asks, "Who if I cried out would hear me among the angelic orders?"

It seems like such an easy question. For believers, the answer is quite simply, "God, that's who." And not just God, but the angels as well. And not just any angel, but *our own personal guardian angel* who, as St. Basil the Great wrote, was created to "protect, guard, and guide" us through life.

While the answer to the question Rilke asked seems obvious (to a believer, at least), how many times have we too felt alone, lost in our worries, or ostracized by those around us? How many of us have asked this very same question? Abandoned to our own experiences, feeling vulnerable and insufficient as we ponder the powerful gravitational forces of our daily lives—our work, our families, our friends, our homes, our health, our finances—when have we questioned whether there was anyone out there who could help us in our times of need?

We can all be assured that along with God in his many forms there is a unique race of beings born of the Divine at the moment of creation, and this race of beings is part of all that is seen and unseen and whose job it is to assist, instruct, and comfort. Enter: the angels.

Catholics believe that from the moment we are conceived until the end of our earthly lives we each have a heavenly protector and shepherd by our side. This can sometimes be hard to believe in our modern technological world because many of us might not feel the presence of the angels in our lives. Yet, most of us are not conscious of the air we breathe that gives us life every day. That doesn't mean that air doesn't exist, does it? It just means we're not aware of the powerful force that surrounds us in everything we do. The same can be said of angels.

Angels are all around us—behind us, in front of us, above and below. You have your guardian angel and the person standing next to you has hers, and the person standing next to her has his. If we could see the way the angels see, we would notice that our world is a very, very crowded place indeed.

It can be difficult to wrap our minds around these angelic protectors. Consider how they have been portrayed in art and movies over the years. There are cherubs in Renaissance paintings, like tiny cupids with smiles and rosy cheeks; there are the illuminated winged beings painted on the covers of greeting and prayer cards; there is Clarence from the perennial Christmas movie *It's a Wonderful Life*, starring Jimmy Stewart. These pleasant images of angels have been ingrained in our collective imagination. And this is a good thing. After all, the nature of angels is that they are invisible by design but have the ability to take shape in ways that are beneficial to our minds and to our lives. These images help ground us and make something so unfamiliar familiar. But the angels of real life are much grander and more commanding than those in pictures and in film. They are awe-inspiring when they make an appearance. As described by Rilke in his poem, "Every angel is terrifying."

Terrifying?

Yes, but only in the way that the birth of a child is terrifying as life as we've known it changes forever. A new world is laid before us. This is why, during most biblical encounters with human beings, the angels say, "Be not afraid." It's not the angels' job to frighten us, but that doesn't mean their brilliance isn't disturbing, especially when they are unveiling a new reality to us. Some of us may have 20/20 vision, but a brush with an angel soon makes us realize that perfect eyesight on earth doesn't mean we're seeing everything that exists.

THE PRESENCE OF ANGELS

Angel comes from the Greek word *angelos*, which itself was derived from the Hebrew word *malakh*, which means "messenger." Their primary job is to lead us to God. They're like mountain guides trained to help us navigate successful treks through our lives. We wouldn't attempt to climb Mount Everest or descend into the Grand Canyon without tapping into the resources offered by trained guides. So too should we avail ourselves of the assistance offered us by the angels.

While the angels appear throughout the Bible, one of the most perplexing of angelic appearances occurs in the Acts of the

Apostles in the narrative concerning Peter, the disciple who famously denied Christ three times. The story takes place just following the death and resurrection of Jesus. Roman authorities have begun persecuting the followers of Christ. The apostles, enflamed with courage from the Holy Spirit, are nonetheless on the run. Stephen has already been martyred while Saul (who will later be struck blind on the road to Damascus and become Paul) looked on with delight. King Herod has captured a number of followers and orders the decapitation of James, the brother of John. Herod then turns his attention to Peter, who remains as the unofficial leader of this group of troublemakers.

> When he had seized him, he put him in prison and handed him over to four squads of soldiers to guard him, intending to bring him out to the people after the Passover. While Peter was kept in prison, the church prayed fervently to God for him. The very night before Herod was going to bring him out, Peter, bound with two chains, was sleeping between two soldiers, while guards in front of the door were keeping watch over the prison. Suddenly an angel of the Lord appeared and a light shone in the cell. He tapped Peter on the side and woke him, saying, "Get up quickly." And the chains fell off his wrists. The angel said to him, "Fasten your belt and put on your sandals." He did so. Then he said to him, "Wrap your cloak around you and follow me." Peter went out and followed him; he did not realize that what was happening with the angel's help was real; he thought he was seeing a vision. After they had passed the first and the second guard, they came before the iron gate leading into the city. It opened

for them of its own accord, and they went outside and walked along a lane, when suddenly the angel left him. Then Peter came to himself and said, "Now I am sure that the Lord has sent his angel and rescued me from the hands of Herod and from all that the Jewish people were expecting." (Acts 12:4–11)

This is a dramatic scene, but read on; the story continues:

As soon as he realized this, he went to the house of Mary, the mother of John whose other name was Mark, where many had gathered and were praying. When he knocked at the outer gate, a maid named Rhoda came to answer. On recognizing Peter's voice, she was so overjoyed that, instead of opening the gate, she ran in and announced that Peter was standing at the gate. They said to her, "You are out of your mind!" But she insisted that it was so. They said, "It is his angel." Meanwhile Peter continued knocking; and when they opened the gate, they saw him and were amazed. He motioned to them with his hand to be silent, and described for them how the Lord had brought him out of the prison. And he added, "Tell this to James and to the believers." Then he left and went to another place. (Acts 12:12–17)

Having an angel break you out of prison and save your life is one thing—God's messengers are known for working miracles. But check out the reaction of the people inside the house after Peter knocks at the door. They find it easier to believe they are looking at Peter's angel than to believe Peter escaped. Astonished, they say, in essence, *That can't be him. It must be his angel.*

Like this happens all the time.

This passage is so wonderfully odd. It implies that angels were so accepted among the general population that they could be taken for granted. It suggests that in first-century Palestine the earthly world and the heavenly world were just a door apart.

How our world would change today if we believed that angels truly walked among us all the time!

So how do we pray with our angelic protectors? One devotion, which has great power but which many people see as almost too childlike to be taken seriously, is the traditional prayer to our guardian angel. I try to recite these words every day, for a few reasons. One, to acknowledge my angelic friend, who is always by my side. Two, to bless the day. And three, to grow in deeper relationship with my personal spiritual body and soul guard. I recommend you commit this prayer to memory:

Angel of God,
my guardian dear,
To whom God's love
commits me here,
Ever this day,
be at my side,
To light and guard,
Rule and guide.
Amen.

Moreover, we can ask your guardian angel to pray *with* us. Too often we forget how powerful and comforting it is to pray with another. We might feel comfortable praying in a church, but many of us are shy about asking another person to pray with us. Yet, we never have to be shy around our angel, so here is a short exercise you can do to invoke and engage your angel during your prayer time.

1. Find a quiet place (but I've been known to do this exercise on a crowded subway).

2. Close your eyes, take a moment to settle yourself, then imagine your guardian angel by your side. You'll know your angel is with you when you begin to feel a sense of peace. Your angel is always with you but sometimes our thoughts and feelings block our awareness.

3. When you're ready, quietly intone: "Guardian angel, pray with me. Lead me closer to God. Protect me and give me direction throughout the day."

4. Reveal to your angel your worries, successes, hopes, and dreams. Ask for guidance and then recite the Lord's Prayer with your angel. Really imagine that your angel is praying those words with you.

5. Remember these words of Jesus: "For where two or three are gathered in my name, there am I in the midst of them" (Matthew 18:20). It's a simple equation: You plus your

angel equals Jesus's presence. Christ is always with you too.

In addition to the guardian angels, there are other beings in heaven who make up the angelic hierarchy. These include seraphim, cherubim, thrones, dominions, virtues, powers, principalities, and archangels. All of these angels have unique attributes and jobs in the universe, but for our purposes we'll focus on the three powerful archangels: Michael, Gabriel, and Raphael, who, in addition to our guardian angel, can assist us in times of need.

What follows are a number of prayers and devotions that we can add to our spiritual toolbox, a way of constructing a life in which we live knowing that no matter how alone we might feel, we've got friends in very special places.

Expanded Prayer to Your Guardian Angel

Angel of God's light, whom God sends as a companion for
    me on earth, protect me from the snares of the devil,
    and help me to walk always as a child of God, my
    Creator.
Angel of God's truth, whose perfect knowledge serves what
    is true, protect me from deceits and temptations. Help
    me to know the truth, and always to live the truth.
Angel of God's love, who praises Jesus Christ, the only Son
    of God, who sacrificed his life for love of us, sustain me
    as I learn the ways of divine love, of sacrificial
    generosity, of meekness and lowliness of heart.

Thank you, my heavenly friend, for your watchful care. At
the moment of my death, bring me to heaven, where the
one true God, who is light, truth, and love, lives and
reigns forever and ever.
Amen.

Prayer to St. Michael for Protection and Guidance

O glorious archangel St. Michael, prince of the heavenly host,
defend us in battle, and in the struggle which is ours against the
principalities and powers, against the rulers of this world of
darkness, against spirits of evil in high places. Come to the aid
of men, whom God created immortal, made in his own image
and likeness, and redeemed at a great price from the tyranny of
the devil.

Fight this day the battle of the Lord, together with the holy
angels, as already thou hast fought the leader of the proud angels,
Lucifer, and his apostate host, who were powerless to resist thee,
nor was there a place for them any longer in heaven. But that
cruel, ancient serpent, who is called the devil or Satan, who se-
duces the whole world, was cast into the abyss with all his angels.

Behold, this primeval enemy and slayer of man has taken
courage. Transformed into an angel of light, he wanders about
with all the multitude of wicked spirits, invading the earth in order to blot out the name of God and of his Christ, to seize upon,
slay, and cast into eternal perdition souls destined for the crown
of eternal glory.

This wicked dragon pours out, as a most impure flood, the
venom of his malice on men of depraved mind and corrupt heart,

the spirit of lying, of impiety, of blasphemy, and the pestilent breath of impurity, and of every vice and iniquity.

These most crafty enemies have filled and inebriated with gall and bitterness the Church, the spouse of the Immaculate Lamb, and have laid impious hands on her most sacred possessions.

In the holy place itself, where has been set up the see of the most holy Peter and the chair of truth for the light of the world, they have raised the throne of their abominable impiety, with the iniquitous design that when the pastor has been struck, the sheep may be scattered.

Arise then, O invincible prince, bring help against the attacks of the lost spirits to the people of God, and bring them the victory.

The Church venerates thee as protector and patron; in thee the holy Church glories as her defense against the malicious powers of this world and of hell; to thee has God entrusted the souls of men to be established in heavenly beatitude.

Oh, pray to the God of peace that he may put Satan under our feet, so far conquered that he may no longer be able to hold men in captivity and harm the Church. Offer our prayers in the sight of the Most High, so that they may quickly conciliate the mercies of the Lord; and beating down the dragon, the ancient serpent, who is the devil and Satan, do thou again make him captive in the abyss, that he may no longer seduce the nations. Amen.

Prayer of St. Raphael for Guidance or Before You Leave on a Trip

Glorious archangel, St. Raphael, great prince of the heavenly court, illustrious for your gifts of wisdom and grace, guide of travelers by land and by sea, consoler of the unfortunate and refuge of sinners, I entreat you to help me in all my needs and in all the trials of this life, as you did once assist the young Tobias in his journeying. And since you are the physician of God, I humbly pray you to heal my soul of its many infirmities and my body of the ills that afflict it, if this favor is for my greater good. I ask, especially, for angelic purity, that I may be made fit to be the living temple of the Holy Spirit.

Prayer to St. Gabriel for Those Lost and Feeling Abandoned, for Those Looking for Direction and Guidance

O blessed archangel Gabriel, we beseech thee, do thou intercede for us at the throne of Divine Mercy in our present necessities, that as thou didst announce to Mary the mystery of the Incarnation, so through thy prayers and patronage in heaven we may obtain the benefits of the same, and sing the praise of God forever in the land of the living. Amen.

Devotions to the Most Holy Angels, Holy Protectors of Humans

Bless the Lord, all you his angels, you who are mighty in strength. And do his will.

Intercede for me at the throne of God and by your unceasing watchfulness protect me from every danger of soul and body.

Obtain for me the grace of final perseverance, so after this life I may be admitted to your glorious company and may sing with you the praises of God for all eternity.

O all you holy angels and archangels, thrones and dominions, principalities and powers and virtues of heaven, cherubim and seraphim and especially you, my dear guardian angel, intercede for me and obtain for me the special favor I now ask.

(State your intention here.)

(Say nine Our Fathers.)

CHAPTER 13

Mary: Our Holy Mother

*Never be afraid of loving the Blessed Virgin too much. You
can never love her more than Jesus did.*

—ST. MAXIMILIAN KOLBE

On a cold Christmas Eve, a seventeen-year-old girl with silky
blond hair and pale blue eyes gave birth to a baby boy. It had been
an unexpected pregnancy that culminated in a difficult delivery,
but as the new mother cradled her newborn, she realized that her
life had changed forever. She was young in years, but as she gazed
down at her baby, she felt a great swelling of protectiveness and
responsibility toward her son. Women dressed in white attended
to the new mother and her newborn until all their immediate
needs had been met, after which the child was whisked away so
that the mother could rest. Exhausted and feeling equally empty
and filled in a way she couldn't yet quite describe, the young
woman looked out the window from her bed. *No snow*, she
thought. *No white Christmas.* She drifted off to sleep.

She awoke later that night, in the predawn hours of Christmas

Day, realized the baby wasn't near, and got out of bed. She walked down the hall, the hospital quiet, the fluorescent light blinding. Somehow, by instinct, she knew where to go, even though she'd never before been in a place like this.

She stopped at the viewing window. Her eyes searched the rows of glass cribs, each one containing a child swaddled in a receiving blanket, their names written in ink on pink and blue index cards attached to the bassinets. She found her son, felt something leap inside her, and watched him sleep beneath the warm stars of electric light. She touched the window that separated her from her child and swore to protect her boy, to raise him right, to honor God, to do whatever she needed to do to make sure that he was safe. She whispered, "I will always love you," and as if the boy heard, he stirred for a moment and then became still.

I don't remember my mom saying those words to me, but I do remember how through the best of times and the worst of times she was unfailingly there to guide and protect me. To make sure that I did my homework and got to school on time. To make certain that I was respectful to God and others. My mother was a deeply religious woman who worked as a housekeeper during the day and at night partnered with my father in doing his upholstering work. I look back now and realize that, especially as our family grew (she gave birth to four daughters, my sisters), she must have been perpetually sleep deprived and stressed. But none of that got through to me then. Through exhaustion and endless hardships, she kept her vow to protect, guide, and support her children. Throughout everything, my mother kept a sincere devotion to Jesus, praying to him every night. She also cultivated a deep prayer relationship with the Blessed Mother, whom she relied upon for guidance during dark nights and challenging days.

My mom isn't much different from billions of other mothers who have fed and cleaned, sacrificed and instructed their own children throughout life. And she's not much different from Jesus's mother, except that the Blessed Virgin Mary was born without sin, gave birth to God, and is the queen of heaven. Okay, those are big differences, but the similarities are strong and the importance of motherhood is sacred. This is why devotions to the Virgin Mary are so popular. She's a mother—a very special mother—but she's also a human being who suffered the pains of childbirth, protected her child from harm when he was a boy and young man, and had to suffer as a witness to her son's brutal execution. She was always with him during the big moments of his life, good and bad.

Love for another is always a mystery, existing in unknown places in our hearts. It is this mysterious love that lies at the heart of one of the most popular devotions in Catholicism, the Rosary.

THE ROSARY

The Rosary is a collection of prayers involving a string of beads that are used to keep track of the numerous Our Fathers and Hail Marys we recite while meditating on certain mysteries of Jesus's and Mary's lives. Each set of prayers is called a decade; we pray five decades to complete a full cycle of the devotion.

Now, mysteries engage our senses and our intellect. They challenge us to solve puzzles, to look, listen, and pay attention to people, places, and situations we may normally overlook. Consider the beloved fictional detective Sherlock Holmes. The keen-eyed sleuth's methodology involved scrutinizing every detail when something had gone afoot. He observed, analyzed, drew connections, used his shrewd acumen, and tapped into his intuition to solve one conundrum after another.

Similarly, we are called to be spiritual detectives when we pray the Rosary. This is a devotion that requires observing and interviewing: talking to bystanders and asking participants to tell us what they know about what happened. The difference between Sherlock's task and ours is that we are not looking for a smoking gun as much as we are asking the primary witness, the Virgin Mary, to reveal to us the secrets of love and mercy that lie behind the life of her son, Jesus.

The Rosary, a contemplative devotion, is a collection of twenty different events in Jesus's life told to us through his mother, Mary. When we talk about point of view in movies and books, we are essentially talking about who is telling the story; while the Rosary has often, mistakenly, been seen as a prayer cycle *to* the Blessed Mother, it is actually about sitting in Mary's presence and having her relate the stories of the most joyful, sorrowful, luminous, and glorious moments in her son's life from her unique point of view as a mom.

I like to think of the Rosary as a scrapbook of an extraordinary life, one that I can look at while sitting side by side with someone who can tell me all about these moments in Jesus's life.

We're going to go through all of the mysteries, one by one, as if they were different scrapbooks. As we turn the pages of each scrapbook, we are shown five spectacular and meaningful scenes that are very important to Mary. These are her son's big moments. She lingers over these pages, commemorating these moments with pride, pain, and motherly love. If we are to connect heart-to-heart with the Blessed Mother as she sits with us and remembers, we need to know what it is she is sharing with us. Here, then, are the four sets of mysteries and the scenes depicted in each.

JOYFUL MYSTERIES

The Annunciation

The Visitation

The Nativity of Jesus Christ

The Presentation of the Infant Jesus in the Temple

The Finding of Jesus at the Temple

The Joyful Mysteries center on the happy early years of Jesus and Mary's life together. In the Annunciation, the angel Gabriel descends upon the young virgin and tells her that she is going to be the mother of the Son of God. In the next scene, the Visitation, Mary visits her cousin Elizabeth, who is also pregnant with a son—John, who will grow up to become the baptist of the desert and prepare the way for Jesus's ministry. The Nativity follows. Here, we are privileged onlookers in a very private moment as Mary gives birth to Jesus. Shepherds and kings are visitors who symbolize the fact that Jesus came into this world for the very poor and the very rich, for locals and strangers, for wanderers and outsiders, for the secure and insecure. The fourth Joyful Mystery takes place eight days after that night when Mary and Joseph present Jesus at the temple, a ritual that was customary in Jewish tradition. There they meet Simeon, who offers a prophecy about the child. The final mystery in this cycle takes place years later. This mystery focuses on Mary and Joseph searching for their son, who they feared was lost but whom they found in the temple preaching to scholars and holy people with the wisdom of someone much older than he.

LUMINOUS MYSTERIES

The Baptism of Jesus in the River Jordan

The Manifestation of Jesus at Cana

The Proclamation of the Kingdom of God

The Transfiguration of Jesus

The Last Supper

The Luminous Mysteries open with the baptism of Jesus in the river Jordan. As cousin John pours water over his body, the Holy Spirit descends in the form of a dove and a voice proclaims, "This is my beloved son in whom I am well pleased." We then move on to the story of the Wedding at Cana. In the middle of a joyful celebration, the wine runs out. Mary urges Jesus to help. He is reluctant but acquiesces and performs his first public miracle by changing water into wine. Afterward, Mary introduces us to her son by proclaiming that the kingdom of God is at hand. In time, we listen in on the Sermon on the Mount, when a new set of commandments known as the Beatitudes are set forth by Jesus the Teacher. The kingdom of God, Jesus is saying, is neither tomorrow nor yesterday; it's here and now. The next story is the Transfiguration, in which the light of God's love shines through his son in the form of a mystical experience: Christ, Moses, and the prophet Elijah meet together high on a mountaintop. Jesus proclaims that he is here not to overthrow the law but to fulfill it. The voice of God booms forth again, saying, "This is my beloved son, listen to him." The Luminous Mysteries end with the Last Supper, when Jesus shares his final meal with his friends and disciples and offers them the bread and wine of life.

THE SORROWFUL MYSTERIES

The Agony in the Garden

The Scourging of Jesus at the Pillar

The Crowning of Jesus with Thorns

The Carrying of the Cross by Christ Jesus

The Crucifixion of Jesus

As we progress through the devotion, we move to the Sorrowful Mysteries. These chronicle Jesus's suffering, Passion, and death. The Agony in the Garden finds Jesus pleading with God to keep him safe from harm and to prevent him from having to suffer the darkness that seems to be crawling toward him. "Father, if you are willing, take this cup from me; yet not my will, but yours be done" (Luke 22:42). The story continues with the Scourging of Jesus at the Pillar, in which Christ is brutally beaten by the Roman authorities. His reputation as a leader is mocked as his tormentors fashion a crown made of spiked thorns and place it on his head. Jesus is then forced to carry his cross, the means of his execution, to the location where he will be executed. The Sorrowful Mysteries conclude with the Crucifixion, as Jesus is nailed to the cross and exposed to the elements for all to see.

THE GLORIOUS MYSTERIES

The Resurrection

The Ascension of Christ Jesus to Heaven

The Descent of the Holy Spirit upon the Apostles

The Assumption of Mary

The Crowning of Mary as the Queen of Heaven

The final set of mysteries is the Glorious Mysteries. The first image we confront is that of the Resurrection. Jesus has risen from the dead and with him rise our hopes for eternal salvation. We move on to the miracle of the Ascension, in which Christ blesses his friends and is taken up to heaven. The mysteries continue with Mary and the apostles receiving the gift of the Holy Spirit and setting out to preach the Good News of the Resurrection. The set concludes with God the Father blessing Mary by assuming her body into heaven and crowning her in glory.

These four groups of mysteries aren't meant to be prayed all in one day, though there are some marathon runner–like spirit practitioners who make this a daily ritual. Instead, you can choose one set of mysteries a day. Traditionally, the Joyful Mysteries are prayed on Mondays and Saturdays, the Sorrowful Mysteries are prayed on Tuesdays and Fridays, the Glorious Mysteries on Wednesdays and Sundays, and the Luminous Mysteries on Thursdays. But, truth be told, you can pray the Rosary anytime you want and focus on a set of mysteries that is resonating in your life at the moment. The Rosary is meant to be an exercise in pondering in your heart the life of Jesus. Though there is a very specific way to perform the devotion (as outlined below), you can pray this devotion anywhere, either alone or in a group, in a church, at home, while waiting in a doctor's office, or when you're out walking your dog.

Praying the Rosary

1. Choose a set of mysteries (the corresponding biblical passages follow these instructions). Make the sign of the cross. Recite the Apostles' Creed while holding the crucifix. If you don't have rosary beads, you can count the prayers on your fingers.

2. On the first bead say an Our Father (the Lord's Prayer).

3. On the three beads that follow, recite a Hail Mary for each and meditate on three virtues: faith, hope, and charity.

4. Recite the Glory Be between your last Hail Mary bead and the next.

5. On the following bead, say an Our Father and then begin meditating on the first mystery.

6. Moving to your right, or counterclockwise, begin praying the Hail Mary. Repeat this prayer for each bead and continue meditating on the mystery.

7. After reciting a Hail Mary on each of the ten beads, recite the Glory Be. This completes the first decade.

8. Repeat steps 5 through 7 for each mystery, continuing along the rosary beads, and conclude your prayer with a Hail, Holy Queen.

9. Finish your Rosary by making the sign of the cross.

What follows are the biblical passages associated with the different stories of the Rosary. I've used these over the years to help me focus my attention on the scene, the characters, the words, and the lessons at the heart of these moments in Jesus's life. I offer them here as a way of entering deeper into the experiences of Jesus and Mary in hopes that you'll encounter comfort, inspiration, joy, and healing. Pay attention to the words. If a particular word or phrase stands out for you, such as "servant" or "your will be done," then carry that with you in your recitation of the Rosary. It's Mary's way of directing your attention to something special between the two of you.

THE FIRST JOYFUL MYSTERY

The Annunciation
In the sixth month the angel Gabriel was sent by God to a town in Galilee called Nazareth, to a virgin engaged to a

man whose name was Joseph, of the house of David. The virgin's name was Mary. And he came to her and said, "Greetings, favored one! The Lord is with you." But she was much perplexed by his words and pondered what sort of greeting this might be. The angel said to her, "Do not be afraid, Mary, for you have found favor with God. And now, you will conceive in your womb and bear a son, and you will name him Jesus. He will be great, and will be called the Son of the Most High, and the Lord God will give to him the throne of his ancestor David. He will reign over the house of Jacob forever, and of his kingdom there will be no end." Mary said to the angel, "How can this be, since I am a virgin?" The angel said to her, "The Holy Spirit will come upon you, and the power of the Most High will overshadow you; therefore the child to be born will be holy; he will be called Son of God. And now, your relative Elizabeth in her old age has also conceived a son; and this is the sixth month for her who was said to be barren. For nothing will be impossible with God." Then Mary said, "Here am I, the servant of the Lord; let it be with me according to your word." Then the angel departed from her.

LUKE 1:26–38

THE SECOND JOYFUL MYSTERY

The Visitation

In those days Mary set out and went with haste to a Judean town in the hill country, where she entered the house of Zechariah and greeted Elizabeth. When Elizabeth heard Mary's greeting, the child leaped in her womb. And Elizabeth was filled with the Holy Spirit and exclaimed with a loud cry, "Blessed are you among women, and blessed is the fruit of your womb. And why has this happened to me, that the mother of my Lord comes to me? For as soon as I heard the sound of your greeting, the child in my womb leaped for joy. And blessed is she who believed that there would be a fulfillment of what was spoken to her by the Lord."

LUKE 1:39–45

THE THIRD JOYFUL MYSTERY

The Nativity of Jesus Christ

In those days a decree went out from Emperor Augustus that all the world should be registered. This was the first registration and was taken while Quirinius was governor of Syria. All went to their own towns to be registered. Joseph also went from the town of Nazareth in Galilee to Judea, to the city of David called Bethlehem, because he was descended from the house and family of David. He went to be registered with Mary, to whom he was engaged and who was expecting a child. While they were there, the time came for her to deliver her child. And she gave birth to her firstborn son and wrapped him in bands of cloth, and laid him in a manger, because there was no place for them in the inn.

LUKE 2:1–7

THE FOURTH JOYFUL MYSTERY

The Presentation of the Infant Jesus in the Temple
When the time came for their purification according to the law of Moses, they brought him up to Jerusalem to present him to the Lord (as it is written in the law of the Lord, "Every firstborn male shall be designated as holy to the Lord"), and they offered a sacrifice according to what is stated in the law of the Lord, "a pair of turtledoves or two young pigeons."

Now there was a man in Jerusalem whose name was Simeon; this man was righteous and devout, looking forward to the consolation of Israel, and the Holy Spirit rested on him. It had been revealed to him by the Holy Spirit that he would not see death before he had seen the Lord's Messiah. Guided by the Spirit, Simeon came into the temple; and when the parents brought in the child Jesus, to do for him what was customary under the law, Simeon took him in his arms and praised God, saying,

"Master, now you are dismissing your servant in peace,
according to your word;
for my eyes have seen your salvation, which you have
prepared in the presence of all peoples,
a light for revelation to the Gentiles
and for glory to your people Israel."

And the child's father and mother were amazed at what was being said about him. Then Simeon blessed them and said to his mother Mary, "This child is destined for the falling and the rising of many in Israel, and to be a sign that will be opposed so that the inner thoughts of many will be revealed—and a sword will pierce your own soul too."

LUKE 2:21–35

THE FIFTH JOYFUL MYSTERY

The Finding of Jesus at the Temple

Now every year his parents went to Jerusalem for the festival of the Passover. And when he was twelve years old, they went up as usual for the festival. When the festival was ended and they started to return, the boy Jesus stayed behind in Jerusalem, but his parents did not know it. Assuming that he was in the group of travelers, they went a day's journey. Then they started to look for him among their relatives and friends. When they did not find him, they returned to Jerusalem to search for him. After three days they found him in the temple, sitting among the teachers, listening to them and asking them questions. And all who heard him were amazed at his understanding and his answers. When his parents saw him they were astonished; and his mother said to him, "Child, why have you treated us like this? Look, your father and I have been searching for you in great anxiety." He said to them, "Why were you searching for me? Did you not know that I must be in my Father's house?" But they did not understand what he said to them. Then he went down with them and came to Nazareth, and was obedient to them. His mother treasured all these things in her heart.

LUKE 2:41–51

THE FIRST LUMINOUS MYSTERY

The Baptism of Jesus in the River Jordan

Then Jesus came from Galilee to John at the Jordan, to be baptized by him. John would have prevented him, saying, "I need to be baptized by you, and do you come to me?" But Jesus answered him, "Let it be so now; for it is proper for us in this way to fulfill all righteousness." Then he consented. And when Jesus had been baptized, just as he came up from the water, suddenly the heavens were opened to him and he saw the Spirit of God descending like a dove and alighting on him. And a voice from heaven said, "This is my son, the Beloved, with whom I am well pleased."

MATTHEW 3:13–17

THE SECOND LUMINOUS MYSTERY

The Manifestation of Jesus at Cana

On the third day there was a wedding in Cana of Galilee, and the mother of Jesus was there. Jesus and his disciples had also been invited to the wedding. When the wine gave out, the mother of Jesus said to him, "They have no wine." And Jesus said to her, "Woman, what concern is that to you and to me? My hour has not yet come." His mother said to the servants, "Do whatever he tells you." Now standing there were six stone water jars for the Jewish rites of purification, each holding twenty or thirty gallons. Jesus said to them, "Fill the jars with water." And they filled them up to the brim. He said to them, "Now draw some out, and take it to the chief steward." So they took it. When the steward tasted the water that had become wine, and did not know where it came from (though the servants who had drawn the water knew), the steward called the bridegroom and said to him, "Everyone serves the good wine first, and then the inferior wine after the guests have become drunk. But you have kept the good wine until now." Jesus did this, the first of his signs, in Cana of Galilee, and revealed his glory; and his disciples believed in him.

JOHN 2:1–11

THE THIRD LUMINOUS MYSTERY

The Proclamation of the Kingdom of God

Now when Jesus heard that John had been arrested, he withdrew to Galilee. He left Nazareth and made his home in Capernaum by the sea, in the territory of Zebulun and Naphtali, so that what had been spoken through the prophet Isaiah might be fulfilled:

"Land of Zebulun, land of Naphtali,
on the road by the sea, across the Jordan, Galilee of the
*   Gentiles—*
the people who sat in darkness
have seen a great light,
and for those who sat in the region and shadow of death
light has dawned."

From that time Jesus began to proclaim, "Repent, for the kingdom of heaven has come near."

MATTHEW 4:12–17

THE FOURTH LUMINOUS MYSTERY

The Transfiguration of Jesus

Now about eight days after these sayings Jesus took with him Peter and John and James, and went up on the mountain to pray. And while he was praying, the appearance of his face changed, and his clothes became dazzling white. Suddenly they saw two men, Moses and Elijah, talking to him. They appeared in glory and were speaking of his departure, which he was about to accomplish at Jerusalem. Now Peter and his companions were weighed down with sleep; but since they had stayed awake, they saw his glory and the two men who stood with him. Just as they were leaving him, Peter said to Jesus, "Master, it is good for us to be here; let us make three dwellings, one for you, one for Moses, and one for Elijah"—not knowing what he said. While he was saying this, a cloud came and overshadowed them; and they were terrified as they entered the cloud. Then from the cloud came a voice that said, "This is my Son, my Chosen; listen to him!" When the voice had spoken, Jesus was found alone. And they kept silent and in those days told no one any of the things they had seen.

LUKE 9:28–36

THE FIFTH LUMINOUS MYSTERY

The Last Supper

Then came the day of Unleavened Bread, on which the Passover lamb had to be sacrificed. So Jesus sent Peter and John, saying, "Go and prepare the Passover meal for us that we may eat it." They asked him, "Where do you want us to make preparations for it?" "Listen," he said to them, "when you have entered the city, a man carrying a jar of water will meet you; follow him into the house he enters and say to the owner of the house, 'The teacher asks you, "Where is the guest room, where I may eat the Passover with my disciples?"' He will show you a large room upstairs, already furnished. Make preparations for us there." So they went and found everything as he had told them; and they prepared the Passover meal.

When the hour came, he took his place at the table, and the apostles with him. He said to them, "I have eagerly desired to eat this Passover with you before I suffer; for I tell you, I will not eat it until it is fulfilled in the kingdom of God." Then he took a cup, and after giving thanks he said, "Take this and divide it among yourselves; for I tell you that from now on I will not drink of the fruit of the vine until the kingdom of God comes." Then he took a loaf of bread, and when he had given thanks, he broke it and gave it to them, saying, "This is my body, which is given for you. Do this in remembrance of me." And he did the same with the cup after supper, saying, "This cup that is poured out for you is the new covenant in my blood. But see, the one who betrays me is with me, and his hand is on the table. For the Son of Man is going as it has been determined, but woe to that one by whom he is betrayed!" Then they began to ask one another which one of them it could be who would do this.

LUKE 22:7–23

THE FIRST SORROWFUL MYSTERY

The Agony in the Garden

Then Jesus went with them to a place called Gethsemane; and he said to his disciples, "Sit here while I go over there and pray." He took with him Peter and the two sons of Zebedee, and began to be grieved and agitated. Then he said to them, "I am deeply grieved, even to death; remain here, and stay awake with me." And going a little farther, he threw himself on the ground and prayed, "My Father, if it is possible, let this cup pass from me; yet not what I want but what you want." Then he came to the disciples and found them sleeping; and he said to Peter, "So, could you not stay awake with me one hour? Stay awake and pray that you may not come into the time of trial; the spirit indeed is willing, but the flesh is weak." Again he went away for the second time and prayed, "My Father, if this cannot pass unless I drink it, your will be done." Again he came and found them sleeping, for their eyes were heavy. So leaving them again, he went away and prayed for the third time, saying the same words. Then he came to the disciples and said to them, "Are you still sleeping and taking your rest? See, the hour is at hand, and the Son of Man is betrayed into the hands of sinners. Get up, let us be going. See, my betrayer is at hand."

MATTHEW 26:36–46

THE SECOND SORROWFUL MYSTERY

The Scourging of Jesus at the Pillar
Pilate spoke to them again, "Then what do you wish me to do with the man you call the King of the Jews?" They shouted back, "Crucify him!" Pilate asked them, "Why, what evil has he done?" But they shouted all the more, "Crucify him!" So Pilate, wishing to satisfy the crowd, released Barabbas for them; and after flogging Jesus, he handed him over to be crucified.

MARK 15:12–15

THE THIRD SORROWFUL MYSTERY

The Crowning of Jesus with Thorns
Then the soldiers led him into the courtyard of the palace (that is, the governor's headquarters); and they called to-

gether the whole cohort. And they clothed him in a purple cloak; and after twisting some thorns into a crown, they put it on him. And they began saluting him, "Hail, King of the Jews!" They struck his head with a reed, spat upon him, and knelt down in homage to him. After mocking him, they stripped him of the purple cloak and put his own clothes on him. Then they led him out to crucify him.

MARK 15:16–20

THE FOURTH SORROWFUL MYSTERY

The Carrying of the Cross by Christ Jesus

So they took Jesus; and carrying the cross by himself, he went out to what is called The Place of the Skull, which in Hebrew is called Golgotha.

As they led him away, they seized a man, Simon of Cyrene, who was coming from the country, and they laid the cross on him, and made him carry it behind Jesus. A great number of the people followed him, and among them were women who were beating their breasts and wailing for him. But Jesus turned to them and said, "Daughters of Jerusalem, do not weep for me, but weep for yourselves and for your children."

JOHN 19:17; LUKE 23:26–28

THE FIFTH SORROWFUL MYSTERY

The Crucifixion of Jesus

Meanwhile, standing near the cross of Jesus were his mother, and his mother's sister, Mary the wife of Clopas, and Mary Magdalene. When Jesus saw his mother and the disciple whom he loved standing beside her, he said to his mother, "Woman, here is your son." Then he said to the disciple, "Here is your mother." And from that hour the disciple took her into his own home.

It was now about noon, and darkness came over the whole land until three in the afternoon, while the sun's light failed; and the curtain of the temple was torn in two. Then Jesus, crying with a loud voice, said, "Father, into your hands I commend my spirit." Having said this, he breathed his last. When the centurion saw what had taken place, he praised God and said, "Certainly this man was innocent." And when all the crowds who had gathered there for this spectacle saw what had taken place, they returned home, beating their breasts. But all his acquaintances, including the women who had followed him from Galilee, stood at a distance, watching these things.

JOHN 19:25–27; LUKE 23:44–49

THE FIRST GLORIOUS MYSTERY

The Resurrection

After the sabbath, as the first day of the week was dawning, Mary Magdalene and the other Mary went to see the tomb. And suddenly there was a great earthquake; for an angel of the Lord, descending from heaven, came and rolled back the stone and sat on it. His appearance was like lightning, and his clothing white as snow. For fear of him the guards shook and became like dead men. But the angel said to the women, "Do not be afraid; I know that you are looking for Jesus who was crucified. He is not here; for he has been raised, as he said. Come, see the place where he lay. Then go quickly and tell his disciples, 'He has been raised from the dead, and indeed he is going ahead of you to Galilee; there you will see him.' This is my message for you." So they left the tomb quickly with fear and great joy, and ran to tell his disciples. Suddenly Jesus met them and said, "Greetings!" And they came to him, took hold of his feet, and worshiped him. Then Jesus said to them, "Do not be afraid; go and tell my brothers to go to Galilee; there they will see me."

MATTHEW 28:1–10

THE SECOND GLORIOUS MYSTERY

The Ascension of Christ Jesus to Heaven

So when they had come together, they asked him, "Lord, is this the time when you will restore the kingdom to Israel?" He replied, "It is not for you to know the times or periods that the Father has set by his own authority. But you will receive power when the Holy Spirit has come upon you; and you will be my witnesses in Jerusalem, in all Judea and Samaria, and to the ends of the earth." When he had said this, as they were watching, he was lifted up, and a cloud took him out of their sight.

ACTS 1:6–9

THE THIRD GLORIOUS MYSTERY

The Descent of the Holy Spirit upon the Apostles
When the day of Pentecost had come, they were all together in one place. And suddenly from heaven there came a sound like the rush of a violent wind, and it filled the entire house where they were sitting. Divided tongues, as of fire, appeared among them, and a tongue rested on each of them. All of them were filled with the Holy Spirit and began to speak in other languages, as the Spirit gave them ability.

ACTS 2:1–4

THE FOURTH GLORIOUS MYSTERY

The Assumption of Mary
A great portent appeared in heaven: a woman clothed with the sun, with the moon under her feet, and on her head a crown of twelve stars.

REVELATION 12:1

THE FIFTH GLORIOUS MYSTERY

The Crowning of Mary as the Queen of Heaven

I will greatly rejoice in the Lord,
my whole being shall exult in my God;
for he has clothed me with the garments of salvation,
he has covered me with the robe of righteousness,
as a bridegroom decks himself with a garland,
and as a bride adorns herself with her jewels.

ISAIAH 61:10

THE MIRACULOUS MEDAL

Sometimes God answers our prayers in such a way that the response literally changes the world.

On the evening of July 19, 1830, just before retiring for the night, a young novice nun named Catherine Labouré prayed to St. Vincent de Paul, asking for his intercession on a particular matter. More than anything in the world, Catherine wanted to see and converse with the Virgin Mary.

That was a pretty bold thing to request and not an easy petition for any saint to satisfy. After all, the Blessed Mother had passed from this earth almost 1,800 years earlier. And yet, with God all things are possible.

Just before midnight, the young woman was awakened by the sound of someone calling her name. Catherine opened her eyes. Standing before her was a child of about five years old bathed in light as if radiating phosphorus. "The Virgin Mary is waiting to see you," said this little messenger. The child, whom the young nun believed to be her guardian angel, led Catherine down a hallway to the convent's chapel. As she walked into the antechamber, there before her was Catherine's heart's delight: the Blessed Virgin, flooded in even more light than the angel by Catherine's side. Young Catherine, shaking at the knees, breathless, gazed upon the vision before her as if she had just been born and was seeing her own mother for the first time. Mary spoke to Catherine, the young nun hanging on every word of this celestial mother–daughter talk. The vision of grace implored Catherine to be obedient to her superiors and to be humble. Mary hinted that a great and important destiny—Catherine's life's purpose—would be revealed to her in due time. The child escorted Catherine back to her room. Warmed by her words and enflamed by the Virgin's presence, Catherine pondered these things in her heart, finally falling asleep.

Four months later, on November 27, 1830, the Virgin Mary came again to visit with Catherine in the night, a bright star in the darkness. This time, in what we might today call a hologram, Mary stood on top of a small planet, crushing a snake beneath her feet. In one hand she held a small globe; rays of light emanated from her other. The small globe, the Virgin Mary said, symbolizes the earth, and the rays represent the love and grace she shines on all who seek her help. Near Mary, Catherine could make out a series of words floating in the air: "O Mary conceived without sin, pray for us who have recourse to you." The Blessed Mother then spoke these words: "Have a medal made according to what I have told you. Those who wear it will be blessed with many graces." The vision before her seemed to turn around and

Catherine saw Mary's plan for the back of the medal: the letter *M* crowned with a cross, which represented the connection between Jesus and Mary; and two hearts, one surrounded by thorns and the other pierced with a sword, the Sacred Heart of Jesus and the Immaculate Heart of Mary, respectively. Around this image were twelve stars, which Catherine was told represented the twelve apostles.

Her young mind racing, her heart enflamed, Catherine went off and pondered this vision—the symbols pregnant with meaning and prophecy—and soon shared her visions with her spiritual adviser and Mother Superior. Though the process wasn't easy and there were numerous obstacles along the way—there were many who wondered if Catherine was crazy—the archbishop, after much deliberating, approved plans for the medal. It was designed and struck in 1832 with an initial printing of fifteen hundred medals. Within seven years more than ten million medals were distributed. By 1876, the year Catherine died, there were estimated to be more than one billion of these medals worn by believers all around the world. To this day it is one of the most popular devotions among Catholics and non-Catholics alike.

I first came across the Miraculous Medal when I was on pilgrimage to Lourdes, France, the holy shrine dedicated to the Virgin Mary and the miraculous events that happened there in the mid-nineteenth century. There, in the red hills of southern France, where the autumn air was cold and the streets always seemed to be wet with rain, I purchased one of these medallions at a local souvenir shop. It was just a small pewter pendant that hung from a thin piece of leather string. I didn't know much about the object at the time, just that it looked kind of cool. Not to mention the store seemed to have hundreds of them—a bestseller, I surmised.

I placed the medal around my neck and walked in the rays of the setting French sun to the grotto to pray. The grotto, a sort of natural indentation on the side of a mountain, was where, in February 1858, fourteen-year-old Bernadette Soubirous had the first of eighteen visions of the Virgin Mary. It was during this time that the Blessed Mother revealed to the young girl her desire for the world to experience the love of her son and to partake in the life-saving waters that flowed in a stream beneath this half cave. Since that time this remote area has become a meeting place and respite for pilgrims, sinners, castaways, and the sick and infirm in search of the miraculous healing waters that were blessed by the Virgin Mary so many years ago.

It was evening. The ground was wet, the sky a mix of indigo and clouds the color of cigarette ash. I wasn't really expecting a miracle; I was just wandering in curiosity, not really having any idea about what I would see or feel, though of course secretly I was hoping to experience an apparition of Mary before my eyes.

I didn't receive a vision that evening, but I may have been given something nearly as special. As I entered the grotto area, I dropped to my knees and lifted my eyes to a statue of the Virgin Mary, maybe six feet tall, set high above me in the recess of the mountain, cloaked in white and cornflower blue, her eyes turned toward heaven. I took a deep breath, closed my eyes, and prayed. I was vaguely aware of the hushed murmurs and shuffling footsteps of dozens of other pilgrims just like me approaching the site in reverence. There were people singing and they sounded like a choir of angels. I entered a state of meditation somewhere between sleep and wakefulness. I don't know how long I was praying, but it must have been for a very long time. At some point I opened my eyes and looked around me. I saw in the distance what had to be at least a thousand wayfarers holding flickering candles in the darkness as they made their careful pilgrimage from the grotto to the church, the Basilica of the Rosary, in another part of the mountains. In the glow of this sacred fire I saw old and young walking hand in hand. I saw people in wheelchairs. I saw people struggling along on crutches. There was a gurney on which lay a man, his nurse by his side. All those faces, those hobbled bodies, the collective faith of all these people made me feel like I was floating on my knees—not necessarily levitating, but the feeling of having my heart lifted up inside me. I started to cry, great sobs that came from somewhere deep inside an ineffable part of me that I didn't even know existed. And it seemed as if I somehow became connected with all of these wanderers searching for their miracles. I touched the medal around my neck. I closed my eyes. I gave thanks to God, Jesus, and the Blessed Mother for delivering me to this moment.

The day after that experience, I went back to the gift shop where I had purchased the medal and found a little booklet that contained the Miraculous Medal novena. In honor of that moment I prayed it over nine days, over the course of my final days in France and on the plane ride home. Some years ago I misplaced the booklet and have not seen it since. But it's a devotion that has been around for many years. You might guess at how precious that prayer was to me as I pondered in my heart the experience I had that night. Please know that I hereby hand it to you with reverence and a prayer that making your own personal journey through this novena is as fulfilling and miraculous as was my journey to Lourdes.

The Miraculous Medal Novena

Recite alone or with a group over nine days.

In the name of the Father and of the Son and of the Holy
Spirit. Amen.

Come, O Holy Spirit, fill the hearts of your
faithful, and kindle in them the fire of your love.
Send forth your Spirit, and they shall be created.
And you shall renew the face of the earth.
Let us pray.
O God, who did instruct the hearts of the faithful by
the light of the Holy Spirit, grant us in the same
Spirit to be truly wise and ever to rejoice in his
consolation, through Jesus Christ our Lord. Amen.

O Mary, conceived without sin, pray for us who have
recourse to you. *(Repeat three times.)*

O Lord Jesus Christ, who have vouchsafed to glorify by
numberless miracles the Blessed Virgin Mary, immaculate
from the first moment of her conception, grant that all
who devoutly implore her protection on earth, may
eternally enjoy your presence in heaven, who, with the
Father and Holy Spirit, live and reign, God, forever
and ever. Amen.

O Lord Jesus Christ, who for the accomplishment of your
greatest works, have chosen the weak things of the

163

world, that no flesh may glory in your sight; and who
for a better and more widely diffused belief in the
Immaculate Conception of your Mother, have wished that
the Miraculous Medal be manifested to St. Catherine
Labouré, grant, we beseech you, that filled with like
humility, we may glorify this mystery by word and work.
Amen.

Memorare

Remember, O most compassionate Virgin Mary, that never
was it known that anyone who fled to your protection,
implored your assistance, or sought your intercession
was left unaided. Inspired with this confidence, we fly
unto you, O virgin of virgins, our Mother; to you we
come; before you we kneel sinful and sorrowful. O Mother
of the Word incarnate, despise not our petitions, but in
your clemency hear and answer them. Amen.

Novena Prayer

O immaculate Virgin Mary, Mother of our Lord Jesus and
our Mother, penetrated with the most lively confidence
in your all-powerful and never failing intercession,
manifested so often through the Miraculous Medal, we
your loving and trustful children implore you to obtain
for us the graces and favors we ask during this novena,
if they be beneficial to our immortal souls, and the

souls for whom we pray.
(Here privately form your petitions.)
You know, O Mary, how often our souls have
been the sanctuaries of your son, who hates iniquity.
Obtain for us also a spirit of prayer and self-denial
that we may recover by penance what we have lost by sin
and at length attain to that blessed abode where you are
the queen of angels and of men. Amen.

An Act of Consecration to Our Lady of the Miraculous Medal

O Virgin Mother of God, Mary Immaculate, we dedicate and
consecrate ourselves to you under the title of Our Lady
of the Miraculous Medal. May this medal be for each one
of us a sure sign of your affection for us and a
constant reminder of our duties toward you. Ever while
wearing it, may we be blessed by your loving protection and
preserved in the grace of your son. O most powerful
virgin, Mother of our Savior, keep us close to you every
moment of our lives. Obtain for us, your children, the
grace of a happy death; so that, in union with you, we
may enjoy the bliss of heaven forever. Amen.

O Mary, conceived without sin, pray for us who have
recourse to you. *(Repeat three times.)*

OUR LADY OF PERPETUAL HELP

The Our Lady of Perpetual Help devotion is based on a fifteenth-century Byzantine icon. In this image painted on wood, Mary is seen holding her baby son, Jesus, while archangels Michael and Gabriel look on, hovering in the air. The two angels are depicted holding the instruments of the child's future death: St. Michael (on the left) holds a spear, the wine-soaked sponge, and the crown of thorns, while St. Gabriel (on the right) holds the cross and the nails. Jesus is represented in contemplation of his future Passion. He is so frightened of his destiny that he has flown quickly into the safety of his mother's arms, one sandal dangling from his foot.

Over the years many miracles have been attested to by those who meditate on this image. Those who flee to Mary in fear, as does the child Jesus in this painting, will never be turned away.

What has always fascinated me about this image is the depth of its symbolism. A picture is worth a thousand words, but a symbol is worth a thousand more. The icon of Our Lady of Perpetual Help isn't just an ornate painting, or a simple representation of the relationship between Mary and Jesus. It's a symbol, and symbols embody the object depicted in a supernatural way. Think of the American flag. It's just a flag, made of colorful cloth, but it is also a symbol of an entire nation. It contains within it all the good and the bad of who we are as a people; it is a repository of our collective experiences. It makes some people feel a sense of pride, while it makes others feel a sense of injustice. The flag reveals a lot about who we are as a country and as individuals. We bring to it our own experiences, whether we are wealthy suburbanites, tired farmers, or descendants of slaves living in housing projects.

I hope that religious icons, for believers, at least, are less polarizing. Gazing upon an icon, especially the Our Lady of Perpetual Help, can be like looking through a window into the divine in our midst, to God in the present moment. It might sound contradictory that a painting more than five hundred years old could tell us much about who we are today, but that's because the icon of Our Lady of Perpetual Help is a symbol of life everlasting, a symbol to remind us that we should never be afraid, that we can always run into the arms of our spiritual mother and be held aloft, and that we will be accompanied by angels.

Life is not easy. We will experience joy and sorrow, elation and pain; that's just the way it is. But Our Lady of Perpetual Help reminds us of the life-healing assistance we can be given if we just ask.

Just ask. Then seek. And then knock. But ask first.

Novena to Our Lady of Perpetual Help

In deep reverence of Our Lady of Perpetual Help, the following prayers to Our Lady are repeated once a day for nine consecutive days:

Behold at your feet, O Mother of Perpetual Help, a wretched sinner who has recourse to you and confides in you. O Mother of Mercy, have pity on me.

I hear you called by all, the refuge and the hope of sinners; be, then, my refuge and my hope.

Assist me, for the love of Jesus Christ; stretch forth your hand to a miserable fallen creature, who recommends himself to you, and who devotes himself to your service forever. I bless and thank Almighty God, who in his mercy has given me this confidence in you, which I hold to be a pledge of my eternal salvation.

It is true, dearest Mother, that in the past I have miserably fallen into sin, because I had not turned to you. I know that with your help, I shall conquer. I know too that you will assist me, if I recommend myself to you; but I fear, dear Mother, that in times of danger, I may neglect to call on you, and thus lose my soul. This grace, then, I ask of you with all the fervor of my soul, that in all the attacks of hell, I may ever have recourse to you.

O Mary help me; O Mother of Perpetual Help, never suffer me to lose my God.

(Say three Hail Marys.)

Mother of Perpetual Help, grant that I may ever invoke your most powerful name, which is the safeguard of the living and the salvation of the dying. O purest Mary, O sweetest Mary, let your name henceforth be ever on my lips. Delay not, O Blessed Lady, to help me whenever I call on you; for, in all my temptations, in all my needs, I shall never cease to call on you, ever repeating your sacred name, Mary!

O, what consolation, what sweetness, what confidence, what emotion fills my soul when I utter your sacred name, or even only think of you! I thank the Lord for having given you, for my good, so sweet, so powerful, so lovely a name. But I will not be content with merely uttering your name; let my love for you prompt me ever to hail you, Mother of Perpetual Help.

(Say three Hail Marys.)

Mother of Perpetual Help, you are the dispenser of all the gifts which God grants to us miserable sinners; and for this end he has made you so powerful, so rich, and so bountiful, in order that you may help us in our misery. You are the advocate of the most wretched and abandoned sinners who have recourse to you; come to my aid, dearest Mother, for I recommend myself to you. In your hands I place my eternal salvation, and to you I entrust my soul. Count me among your most devoted servants; take me under your protection, and it is enough for me. For, if you protect me, dear Mother, I fear nothing; not from my sins, because you will obtain for me the pardon of them from Jesus your divine son. But one thing I fear, that in the hour of temptation, I may through negligence fail to have recourse to you and thus perish miserably.

Obtain for me, therefore, the pardon of my sins, love for Jesus, final perseverance, and the grace to have recourse to you and [mention your request], O Mother of Perpetual Help.

(Say three Hail Marys.)

Pray for us, O Mother of Perpetual Help, that we may be made worthy of the promises of Christ.

Let us pray:

Lord Jesus Christ who gave us your Holy Mother Mary, whose renowned image we venerate, to be a Mother ever ready to help us, grant, we beseech you, that we who constantly implore her maternal aid may merit to enjoy perpetually the fruits of your redemption, who lives and reigns with God forever and ever. Amen.

OUR LADY OF MOUNT CARMEL

As a Catholic, I can say that Catholics are weird. I'm sure millions if not billions of non-Catholics (and some of my Catholic brothers and sisters) would agree. We have some strange traditions, one being the Brown Scapular of Our Lady of Mount Carmel.

As I mentioned earlier, a scapular consists of two stamplike pieces of cloth connected by ribbon or string that you wear over your shoulders, with one panel resting over your heart area and the other on your back. Most people wear the scapular underneath their clothes, though I've know some who wear it for all to see, a practice that usually draws quizzical looks.

The Brown Scapular is a devotion based on the spirituality of the Carmelites, a religious order of monastics dating back to the Crusades who originally lived on Mount Carmel in Israel, near what is now Haifa. This community of friars (and, later, nuns) developed a devotion to Jesus's mother and would spend their lives in prayer and meditation. Eventually the order expanded out of the Holy Land, moved across Europe, and spread all around the world. St. John of the Cross, St. Teresa of Ávila, and St. Thérèse of Lisieux were Carmelites whose lives were centered on prayer.

The Brown Scapular is a tool for contemplation. Given to St. Simon Stock in a vision of the Virgin Mary in 1251 as a reminder to the world to call on the Virgin Mary during times of need, the object holds no power in itself beyond being a compelling reminder of God's love for us, as well as helping to focus our attention on heavenly concerns. We wear the scapular to remember to keep God in our heads and in our hearts, and to remember that Jesus and his mother are always in front of us even as they always have our backs.

Scapulars are easy to find online and at religious stores. This petitionary novena is meant to be prayed while wearing the scapular, but it can be prayed without one. The most important part of the prayer is the simple turning of our attention on the Blessed Mother during our time of need.

Novena to Our Lady of Mount Carmel

First Day

O beautiful flower of Carmel, most fruitful vine, splendor of heaven, holy and singular, who brought forth the Son of God, still ever remaining a pure virgin, assist us in our necessity! O star of the sea, help and protect us! Show us that you are our Mother!

(Mention your personal petition here.)

Say the Our Father, a Hail Mary, and a Glory Be.

Our Lady of Mount Carmel, pray for us.

Second Day

Most Holy Mary, our Mother, in your great love for us you gave us the Holy Scapular of Mount Carmel, having heard the prayers of your chosen son St. Simon Stock. Help us now to wear it faithfully and with devotion. May it be a sign to us of our desire to grow in holiness.

(Mention your personal petition here.)

Say the Our Father, a Hail Mary, and a Glory Be.

Our Lady of Mount Carmel, pray for us.

Third Day

O queen of heaven, you gave us the scapular as an outward sign by which we might be known as your faithful children.

May we always wear it with honor by avoiding sin and imitating your virtues. Help us to be faithful to this desire of ours.

(Mention your personal petition here.)
Say the Our Father, a Hail Mary, and a Glory Be.
Our Lady of Mount Carmel, pray for us.

Fourth Day

When you gave us, gracious lady, the scapular as our habit, you called us to be not only servants but also your own children.

We ask you to gain for us from your son the grace to live as your children in joy, peace, and love.

(Mention your personal petition here.)
Say the Our Father, a Hail Mary, and a Glory Be.
Our Lady of Mount Carmel, pray for us.

Fifth Day

O Mother of fair love, through your goodness, as your children, we are called to live in the spirit of Carmel. Help us to live in charity with one another, prayerful as Elijah of old, and mindful of our call to minister to God's people.

(Mention your personal petition here.)
Say the Our Father, a Hail Mary, and a Glory Be.
Our Lady of Mount Carmel, pray for us.

Sixth Day

With loving provident care, O Mother most amiable, you covered us with your scapular as a shield of defense against the Evil One.

Through your assistance, may we bravely struggle

against the powers of evil, always open to your son,
Jesus Christ.

(Mention your personal petition here.)

Say the Our Father, a Hail Mary, and a Glory Be.

Our Lady of Mount Carmel, pray for us.

Seventh Day

O Mary, help of Christians, you assured us that
wearing your scapular worthily would keep us safe from
harm. Protect us in both body and soul with your
continual aid. May all that we do be pleasing to your son
and to you.

(Mention your personal petition here.)

Say the Our Father, a Hail Mary, and a Glory Be.

Our Lady of Mount Carmel, pray for us.

Eighth Day

You give us hope, O Mother of mercy, and through
your scapular promise we might quickly pass through
the fires of purgatory to the kingdom of your son.

Be our comfort and our hope. Grant that our hope
may not be in vain but that, ever faithful to your son
and to you, we may speedily enjoy after death the
blessed company of Jesus and the saints.

(Mention your personal petition here.)

Say the Our Father, a Hail Mary, and a Glory Be.

Our Lady of Mount Carmel, pray for us.

Ninth Day

O Most Holy Mother of Mount Carmel, when asked by a saint to grant privileges to the family of Carmel, you gave assurance of your motherly love and help to those faithful to you and to your son.

Behold us, your children. We glory in wearing your holy habit, which makes us members of your family of Carmel, through which we shall have your powerful protection in life, at death, and even after death.

Look down with love, O gate of heaven, on all those now in their last agony!

Look down graciously, O virgin, flower of Carmel, on all those in need of help!

Look down mercifully, O Mother of our Savior, on all those who do not know that they are numbered among your children.

Look down tenderly, O queen of all saints, on the poor souls!

(Mention your personal petition here.)

Say the Our Father, a Hail Mary, and a Glory Be.

Our Lady of Mount Carmel, pray for us.

CHAPTER 14

Jesus: Our Beloved

I serve a higher power, Jesus Christ. I make no apologies in
saying that.

—RICK WARREN

I was introduced to the devotion of the Most Holy Name of Jesus
quite by accident one early autumn evening in a tiny apartment in
Florence, Italy. Weeks before, I had been a mild-mannered assis-
tant editor at a prestigious publishing company in New York, and
then suddenly I decided that I had to answer a call to travel to Europe and spend forty days and forty nights in solitude searching
for God. Whether that calling was just youthful folly, a figment of
my imagination, or the voice of God speaking to me I just don't
know, but at some point I got the idea in my head to leave everything behind and seek God in various shrines and sacred places
throughout Italy, Austria, Poland, the Czech Republic, and France.

But there was a catch. I had very little money. I had roughly
one thousand dollars and it had to last for one month and ten
days. There was no way that my anxious parents, who were only a

couple of years past a divorce and struggling to find their own way, were able to bankroll my little fit of insanity. To them, backpacking through Europe was a rich kid's game, something other people's children did after graduating from college. But I had earned my degree almost five years earlier and was closing in on a promotion at my dream job. What was I thinking? Still, there was something inside me telling me to go. So with little more than a basic inkling that it was now or never, I resigned from my job and within a couple of weeks had taken up residence in the small bedroom of a boardinghouse just outside Florence.

Florence. I had always dreamt of visiting this city. This was the capital of the Renaissance, home of Michelangelo and da Vinci and my literary hero, Dante Alighieri, who had been born there at the close of the Middle Ages. It would not be a stretch to say that it was Dante's *Divine Comedy* that had lured me to Florence. In order to feel less guilty about my decision to abandon security just to roam Europe, I had concocted a half-true story that I was going to study this classic work in the poet's hometown. I did bring a dog-eared copy of *The Inferno* with me and signed up for a few inexpensive Italian lessons, but that was it. My main objective was to visit the Duomo and museums such as the Uffizi, then head to Rome to visit the Vatican, after which I anticipated a few more stops on my way to Lourdes, France, where I would drink the holy water of miracles and bring some back for my family, which seemed to be falling apart at the seams.

But I was miserable in Florence. I was homesick. Frightened. And wracked with insecurity and shame for being unemployed and on an extended no-frills vacation (if you could call living in cheap boardinghouses and hostels with maybe a meal and a half per day a vacation). For the first time in my life since the age of twelve I did not have a job; coming from a family in which work was what defined you as a person, this meant that I was living without any definition.

On one particular night, after having been in Italy for almost a week, I arrived back in my eight-by-eight-foot room, where the door banged the bed every time I entered or departed. I had been walking all day, visiting churches, praying, and reading Dante as I strolled the cobblestone streets of Via dei Calzaiuoli. Tired and hungry, I lay down on the bed and stared up at the ceiling. A few moments later, I heard what sounded like someone tuning a radio in the hall. I heard strange voices, lots of static, lots of noise. After a minute or two I got off the bed and slowly opened my door to see what was happening outside my room. Astonishingly, no one was there. The corridor was silent as a tomb. I closed the door, paced as much as was possible in such tight quarters, placed my ear against each wall, and peered out my window, which overlooked a quiet courtyard. Nothing.

Except that I could still hear the noise. It was so close. As I stood there trying to figure out where it was coming from, I realized it was coming from me.

What I mean by this is that there was something odd going on inside me. It was almost as if there were a couple of tiny people in my ears and they were arguing and crinkling paper at the same time.

What the heck is going on? I said to myself. I thought maybe a bug had crawled into my ear and was gnawing away at my nerves. But it wasn't a physical thing. I was hearing voices inside my head and, as far as I could tell, they didn't belong to me.

Soon thereafter I started to get nauseated, literally sick to my stomach. *Oh my God*, I thought. *What's wrong with me? Am I go-*

ing crazy? The voices hidden in static, indecipherable arguing, got louder. I started to panic and I couldn't tell if there were angels and demons in my head, if I was losing my mind, or I was suffering hallucinations from lack of food (I hadn't eaten anything since early that morning) or from food poisoning.

I lay back down on the bed, assumed the fetal position, tried like mad to quiet whatever was in my head, and after a few minutes, I started repeating Jesus's name over and over again.

Jesus, Jesus, Jesus.

Jesus, Jesus, Jesus.

Jesus, Jesus, Jesus.

At some point I must have fallen asleep. As far as I can remember, I didn't dream, but when I awoke the next morning my first awareness was that my lips were still mouthing the name of Jesus. I lay on the bed for a few moments, eyeing the room. The noise inside my head was gone. I sat up. I didn't feel sick. In fact, I felt better than I ever had in my life! At that moment I had never felt more focused or alert. Something seemed to be coursing through me, and that something was not crinkly noise pollution. It was something else entirely. It was, I've come to understand many years later, a pure and unadulterated faith. It was as if something had been purged from me that night and now I had arrived in the presence of God. I felt like Jesus was all around me.

While I may very well write a memoir sometime in the future about my pilgrimage through Europe, I will just say here that the remainder of my trip was characterized by a trust that everything would work out, that I was there for a reason, and that God would have my back. Jesus became my companion on that trip. And you know what? Once I surrendered myself to trusting God and realized that Jesus was only two syllables away, everything worked out for me. When I got lost, someone always appeared who guided me where I needed to go. When I was hungry, strangers appeared who offered me food. In Poland, where crushing loneliness struck me hard, I ran into a group of Americans who lived three towns away from my home on Long Island, and we spent the day hanging out together. It was as if the simple name of Jesus was a spiritual superantibiotic that cured worry and fear.

It was only years later that I found out that the word I whispered over and over that terrifying night in Florence was in fact a prayer in itself. It is a special devotion known as the Most Holy Name of Jesus. It is by far the simplest devotion of all, one that focuses on the power of Jesus's name to bless and protect us and help form our lives. The instruction to invoke Jesus's name in prayer and during times of struggle comes from Christ himself: "I will do whatever you ask in my name, so that the Father may be glorified in the Son. If in my name you ask me for anything, I will do it" (John 14:13–14).

Sure, I had heard and read that passage many times throughout the years, but I didn't consciously think that merely uttering Jesus's name would help me that night. At that time in my life my prayers were very wordy. I was in the habit of spilling my thoughts and ideas all over God and out they poured, like M&M's tumbling from a bag that had been ripped open by someone using too much force.

I still pray a lot, but I don't use nearly as many words. These days, I have different devotions that I do all the time, but my favorite prayer is simply the Most Holy Name of Jesus. I recite it over and over again throughout the day. Jesus. Jesus. Jesus. That's it. I just repeat the name of Jesus when I wake in the morning and before I go to bed at night, when I'm dressing and eating, while I'm walking to work or preparing for meetings, when I'm standing in line at a store, and even when I'm working out. (Side note: In the past couple of years I've discovered the joys of weight lifting, and when I work out I sometimes picture Jesus helping me push out the last couple of reps. Try it. It works.) When I'm stressed out, I just take a deep breath and say to myself, *Jesus*. Often I touch my heart when I say his name. Some people at work might suspect me of suffering from heartburn, but really I'm just praying.

Jesus's name carries with it great power. St. Peter knew this when he cured the sick just by saying his friend's name, as we see in this passage from the Acts of the Apostles:

One day Peter and John were going up to the temple at the hour of prayer, at three o'clock in the afternoon. And a man lame from birth was being carried in. People would lay him daily at the gate of the temple called the Beautiful Gate so that he could ask for alms from those entering the temple. When he saw Peter and John about to go into the temple, he asked them for alms. Peter looked intently at him, as did John, and said, "Look at us." And he fixed his attention on them, expecting to receive something from them. But Peter said, "I have no silver or gold, but what I have I give you; in the name of Jesus Christ of Nazareth, stand up and walk." And he took him by the right hand and raised him up; and immediately his feet and ankles were made strong. Jumping up, he stood and began to walk, and he entered the temple with them, walking and leaping and praising God. All the people saw him walking and praising God, and they recognized him as the one who used to sit and ask for alms at the Beautiful

Gate of the temple; and they were filled with wonder and amazement at what had happened to him. (Acts 3:1–10)

We are baptized, married, and die in the name of Jesus. Saints have cast out demons merely by speaking his name. Some people will say words are cheap, but in this case, the holy name is truly priceless. Clearly, Peter understood this truth. You can't deposit it in a bank, but the name of Jesus has been known to make the lame rise and walk.

St. Augustine, St. Bernard, St. Dominic, and St. Francis of Assisi (to name just a few) had a special devotion to the name of Jesus. Each held the name in the highest regard, repeating it over and over again. Friar Thomas of Celano wrote of St. Francis that he was so taken by the name, he "was always occupied with Jesus; Jesus he carried in his heart; Jesus in his mouth . . . in his eyes . . . in his ears . . . in his hands. . . ." St. Francis seemed to carry the name of Jesus so much inside him that he would later bear the five wounds of Christ and exhibit the stigmata.

Now, I'm not saying that all of us need go that far. Bleeding wounds from our palms really isn't the objective here. The point is that replacing our scattered thoughts with the Most Holy Name of Jesus can be transformative. Think of this: How would your life be different if the majority of the thoughts you harbored all day were focused on something life-affirming? When we are going through challenging times or are suffering through loss and illness, heeding St. Paul's advice to "Pray ceaselessly" would be beneficial. We can do this in a profound way simply by speaking the name of Jesus over and over and over again. When we do, we cross the threshold of the Beautiful Gate and experience life everlasting in our earthly lives.

THE DEVOTION

Repeat the name of Jesus as often as you can. Imagine the word being spoken in your heart, the harbor of the Son, and allow it to move throughout your body. Repeat the Most Holy Name throughout the day, bow your head in reverance when you can, and remember never to use the name of Jesus in vain. Refrain from using the name of Jesus when you stub your toe or make a mistake at work. Honor the name and allow it to beat in you as your heart beats in your very chest. This devotion is not to be used as a magic formula but is to be held in reverence.

In addition to this prayer there are two novenas that can be prayed over the course of nine days in honor of the Most Holy Name.

Novena in Honor of the Most Holy Name of Jesus

O Merciful Jesus, who didst in thy early infancy commence thy office of Savior by shedding thy precious blood, and assuming for us that name which is above all names; we thank thee for such early proofs of thine infinite love. We venerate thy sacred name, in union with the profound respect of the angel who first announced it to the earth, and unite our affections to the sentiments of tender devotion which the adorable name of Jesus has in all ages enkindled in the hearts of thy saints.

Animated with a firm faith in thy unerring word, and penetrated with confidence in thy mercy, we now most humbly remind thee of the promise thou hast made, that where two or three should assemble in thy name, thou thyself wouldst be in the midst of them. Come, then, into the midst of us, most amiable Jesus, for it is in thy sacred name we are here assembled; come into our hearts, that we may be governed by thy holy spirit; mercifully grant us, through that adorable name, which is the joy of heaven, the terror of hell, the consolation of the afflicted, and the solid ground of our unlimited confidence, all the petitions we make in this novena.

Oh! Blessed Mother of our Redeemer! Who didst participate so sensibly in the sufferings of thy dear son when he shed his sacred blood and assumed for us the name of Jesus, obtain for us, through that adorable name, the favors we petition in this novena.

Beg also, that the most ardent love may imprint on our hearts that sacred name, that it may be always in our minds and frequently on our lips; that it may be our defense and our refuge in the temptations and trials of life, and our consolation and support in the hour of death. Amen.

Novena in Honor of the Most Holy and Adorable Name of Jesus

JESUS! O name of Jesus! Sweet name! Delightful name!
  Consoling name!
For what else is Jesus than Savior! Therefore, O Jesus, for thy
  sweet name's sake,
be to me a Jesus, and save me. Suffer me not to be eternally
  lost. O good Jesus!
Let not my iniquities destroy me, whom thy bounty made. O
  sweet Jesus!
Recognize in me what is thine, and efface all that is not
  thine.

O sweet Jesus! Show mercy now in the time of mercy, and
    condemn me not in the day of justice.

What profit to thy precious blood, or what honor will my
    destruction give thy holy name, O Jesus!

"The dead shall not praise Thee, O Lord Jesus! Nor all they
    that go down to hell."

Most amiable Jesus! Most meek, most loving Jesus! O Jesus,
    Jesus, Jesus!

Admit me to the number of thy elect.

O Jesus, salvation of those who believe in thee! Comfort of
    those who fly to thee!

O Jesus, Son of the Virgin Mary! Give me grace, wisdom,
    charity, purity, and humility,

that I may love thee perfectly, praise thee, enjoy thee, serve
    thee,

and be glorified in thee, with all those who call upon thy
    name,

Thy holy name, thy sweet name—Jesus. Amen.

THE SACRED HEART OF JESUS

Popularized in the seventeenth century by French Catholic mystic St. Margaret Mary Alacoque, the image of the Sacred Heart of Jesus can be, to the uninitiated, a bit bizarre and macabre. In this image, Jesus is usually depicted with an exposed heart that has been pierced with an arrow and is encircled by vines of entwined thorns. Flames emanate from the crown of the heart and the heart itself is sometimes crowned with a cross. This image represents the holy sacred fire, the fire of love and longing for another. Just as two young people can yearn for each other, never wanting to be away from one another, Jesus's exposed heart yearns for all of us. The thorns represent the pain and suffering he experienced on our behalf before he was crucified. The cross is, of course, a symbol of his death and resurrection. The light emanating from the heart symbolizes Christ's love for everyone who gazes upon this image and who meditates on its sacred mysteries.

Raised in poverty, Margaret Mary developed a deep devotion to Jesus. At a young age, she began having visions of Christ. He came to her in consolation during times of crisis, especially after she lost her father when she was eight years old. Preferring prayer and solitude to the trappings of material life, Margaret Mary entered a convent in 1671, at the age of twenty-four. In 1673 she began having regular visions of Jesus; in time, he shared with her a private revelation about his sacred heart. It was Sister Margaret Mary's job to inform and remind people of the world about God's love, mercy, grace, and compassion while she brought to them a vision of Jesus's most holy sacred heart.

I first came across the Sacred Heart as a boy. My mother was a devout woman and she kept a number of images of Jesus around the house as constant reminders of God's presence in our lives. She had one particular image of Jesus with his burning, sacred heart exposed for all of us to see. It was a five-by-seven picture superimposed on a blue background that was frayed and worn at the edges. In my young mind I thought about this image as if it were a school photo, and for years I imagined Jesus posing for his picture in the school gymnasium or in a Sears studio somewhere on Long Island.

That image brings back fond memories. I recall Jesus with a half smile on his face, his exposed chest allowing light to radiate from his heart. That light made me feel safe and warm. Often, when my parents argued, I would remove this picture from its perch in our den and keep it close. Somehow, I felt protected, as if nothing could harm me so long as that picture was in my possession.

During my twenties and thirties I suffered from cluster migraines. The best way to describe a cluster migraine is that it is super painful and it frequently made me feel dizzy and nauseated. These headaches, known as the granddaddy of all migraines, are frighteningly painful. For many years I told people that it felt as if someone were stabbing me in the eye with an ice pick. Much later, I discovered that other cluster migraine sufferers use the exact same imagery to describe the pain. These headaches "cluster" together over a week's time. A victim might suffer a series of headaches over the course of a few days, only to have them vanish for up to year or two and then return with a vengeance just as suddenly as they vanished.

The weekend I met Father How Big Is Your God, I got hit with one of those suckers. I found myself pacing my room, trying my best to take my mind off the pain. In my room was a prayer card featuring the Sacred Heart, and after doing a set of push-ups (for some strange reason, exercise would temporarily ease some of the pain) I gazed upon the image and began repeating to myself the Sacred Heart prayer printed on the back of the card. *Sacred Heart of Jesus I trust in thee. Sacred Heart of Jesus I trust in thee.* Over and over again I repeated these words, even while I was on the verge of throwing up. Clusters can last up to a couple of hours, but that day the pain subsided within fifteen to twenty minutes. Coincidence that I prayed this prayer and that I felt better in record time? I don't think so. Don't get me wrong, I am not endorsing prayer over medical treatment if that is what is necessary. That being said, I would add that combining prayer and medicine is never a bad thing. At any rate, I had suffered cluster migraines for many years, and this unusually quick recovery was something I had never experienced before. I do believe that focusing on Jesus's Sacred Heart and his healing love allowed my body to be healed sooner rather than later. Just as a parent would want to help a child struggling with a fever by applying cold compresses to a forehead, Jesus wants to help us during our time of greatest need.

During one of Sister Margaret Mary Alacoque's visions, Jesus revealed to her twelve promises that are connected to devotion to the Sacred Heart:

1. The promise to bestow upon us all the necessary graces we need in life.

2. The promise to bring peace to our home life.

3. The promise to comfort those who are troubled, sick, or afflicted.

4. The promise to secure safe haven for us in this life and in death.

5. The promise to bless us abundantly in all that we do.

6. The promise of mercy to sinners.

7. The promise that the lukewarm will become enflamed with holy fire.

8. The promise ardent believers will move closer to high perfection in their daily lives.

9. The promise to bless every place in which the image of the Sacred Heart is present and venerated.

10. The promise that priests will have the ability to soften the hard-hearted.

11. The promise that all of those who stay true to the devotion will have their names written in Jesus's heart.

12. The promise of a special blessing to those who receive Holy Communion on the first Fridays over nine consecutive months. Those who honor this request will find safe passage in their final moments of life.

Since that time, the prayer of the Sacred Heart has been a core part of my spiritual devotional toolbox, a constant reminder that divine love protects and heals.

Devotion

Visualize the image of the Sacred Heart, or if you have an actual picture of it, use it as your focal point. Focus on the image and envision Jesus's heart becoming one with yours. Allow them to beat together. Allow the Sacred Heart to give you strength and healing. Repeat the words, "Sacred Heart of Jesus, I trust in thee," for a couple of minutes and then return to your daily life. Keep those words in your heart throughout the day and say them whenever you can.

There is also an extended version of this prayer that you can incorporate into your day-to-day life:

O Sacred Heart of Jesus, I place my trust in thee,
Whatever may befall me, Lord, though dark the hour may be;
In all my woes, in all my joys, though naught but grief I see,
O Sacred Heart of Jesus, I place my trust in thee.
When those I loved have passed away, and I am sore
    distressed,
O Sacred Heart of Jesus, I fly to thee for rest.
In all my trials, great or small, my confidence shall be
Unshaken as I cry, dear Lord, I place my trust in thee.
This is my one sweet prayer, dear Lord, my faith, my trust,
    my love,
But most of all in that last hour, when death points up above,
O sweet savior, may thy face smile on my soul all free.
Oh may I cry with rapturous love, I've placed my trust in
    thee.

Novena to the Sacred Heart of Jesus
(to Be Recited over Nine Days)

O my Jesus, you have said: "Truly I say to you, ask and you will receive, seek and you will find, knock and it will be opened to you." Behold I knock, I seek, and ask for the grace of [name your request].

Say an Our Father, a Hail Mary, and a Glory Be.

Sacred Heart of Jesus, I place all my trust in you.

O my Jesus, you have said: "Truly I say to you, if you ask anything of the Father in my name, he will give it to you." Behold, in your name, I ask the Father for the grace of [name your request].

Say an Our Father, a Hail Mary, and a Glory Be

Sacred Heart of Jesus, I place all my trust in you.

O my Jesus, you have said: "Truly I say to you, heaven and earth will pass away but my words will not pass away." Encouraged by your infallible words, I now ask for the grace of [name your request].

Say an Our Father, a Hail Mary, and a Glory Be

Sacred Heart of Jesus, I place all my trust in you.

O Sacred Heart of Jesus, for whom it is impossible not to have compassion on the afflicted, have pity on us miserable sinners and grant us the grace which we ask of you, through the sorrowful and immaculate heart of Mary, your tender Mother and ours.

Recite the Hail, Holy Queen *(see page 233)*.

St. Joseph, foster father of Jesus, pray for us. Amen.

THE JESUS PRAYER

I first came across the Jesus Prayer not in a book of Scripture or meditations but in the pages of J. D. Salinger's *Franny and Zooey* (1961). In this story, Franny and Zooey are a sister and brother having an extended conversation about the meaning of life. Franny admits to her brother she has been reading *The Way of a Pilgrim*, a nineteenth-century text about a Russian wayfarer on a spiritual quest. This wanderer relates how he met a holy man who taught him how to pray without ceasing by reciting and internalizing the words, "Lord Jesus Christ have mercy on me, a sinner." Franny tells Zooey that she has been using the meditation and has felt something change in her heart.

At first I thought Salinger had made up the prayer, but after doing a little research I found that the Jesus Prayer is a legitimate devotion, a spiritual practice that originated among the Desert Fathers, a group of Christian ascetics who lived in the arid regions of Egypt during the fifth century. While the prayer grew in popularity in the Eastern Orthodox Church, it didn't gain favor in the West until the publication of *The Way of a Pilgrim*. It is now a staple in the lives of many seekers, Catholic and non-Catholic alike.

The anonymous author of the book describes the Jesus Prayer as "a continuous, uninterrupted call on the holy name of Jesus Christ with the lips, mind, and heart; and in the awareness of His abiding presence it is a plea for his undertakings, in all places, at all times, even in sleep. . . . Anyone who becomes accustomed to this prayer will experience great comfort as well as the need to say it continuously. He will become accustomed to it in such a degree that he will not be able to do without it and eventually the Prayer will of itself flow in him."

Part of the power of the prayer lies in its repetition. As with the Most Holy Name and the Prayer of the Sacred Heart, we don't say the Jesus Prayer just once; we repeat it a hundred times, a thousand times, ten thousand times. It can be prayed before we go to sleep, in the moments after we wake up, when we're waiting at a traffic light or standing in line at a grocery store.

In his book *Reaching Out*, beloved spiritual writer Henri Nouwen, a major proponent of the prayer, described the practice in this way:

> The Jesus prayer . . . is meant to be a help to gently empty our minds from all that is not God, and offer all the room to him and him alone. But that is not all. Our prayer be-

comes a prayer of the heart when we have localized in the center of our inner being the empty space in which our God-filled mind can descend and vanish, and where the distinctions between thinking and feeling, knowing and experience, ideas and emotions are transcended, and where God can become our host. "The Kingdom of God is within you" (Luke 17:21) Jesus said. The prayer of the heart takes these words seriously. When we empty our mind from all thoughts and our hearts from all experiences, we can prepare in the center of our innermost being the home for the God who wants to dwell in us. Then we can say with St. Paul, "I live now not with my own life but with the life of Christ who lives in me" (Galatians 2:20). Then we can affirm Luther's words, "Grace is the experience of being delivered from experience." And then we can realize that it is not we who pray, but the Spirit of God who prays in us.

At the heart of these three devotions—the Most Holy Name, the Sacred Heart of Jesus, and the Jesus Prayer—is the experience of being delivered from experience. The name of Jesus lifts us up in times of struggle and heartache, when we feel most like outsiders to the world and to ourselves. Like Mother Teresa, who literally lifted people from the gutters, Jesus's name raises us up, not on a cross, but on his shoulders. We are like children in his arms, and this lifting up gives us a new vantage point, a way of seeing what we could not see before we experienced the love that moves the moon and the stars. We are delivered from experience by being set free from our worries and concerns.

Devotion

Try to settle your mind and body and focus your attention on your heart. Repeat the words, "Lord Jesus Christ, have mercy on me, a sinner," and hear them emanating not from your mind or your mouth but from your heart.

STATIONS OF THE CROSS

The Way of the Cross

When I was a boy, my father, a blue-collar, working-class joe from Long Island, wanted to be a farmer. I, a lanky, bushy-haired, suburban youth with a penchant for Springsteen and Ramones records and Green Lantern and Batman comic books, did not. While my dad dreamt of open country, big sky, and John Deere tractors, I was perfectly content with a skyline crowded with asphalt-shingled rooftops, hanging out with my friends after school, and riding my trusty old metallic purple Schwinn bicycle to Brower Candy Store, where I played video games such as *Dragon's Lair* and *Pole Position* (about that purple bike . . . come on, man, cut me some slack. It was the '80s).

When I was around thirteen years old my parents bought a few acres of farmland in upstate New York. Like me, my mom had little interest in the property, but my father was elated. As a carpenter and upholsterer by day and a repairman and delivery guy by night—usually clocking in seventy to eighty hours a week—my father saw this rural oasis as a respite from the pressures, fumes, traffic, and congestion that characterized his everyday routine. So on weekends he would drag me from our home in Rockville Centre and drive the two of us three hours away to the boonies for fresh air and a change of scenery. To say I was not thrilled about these trips would be an understatement.

Come Saturday mornings I would invariably say good-bye to my mom and sisters and we'd set off in my dad's white Ford van complete with Pergament shag carpet covering rust holes in the floor. The combination of noisy highway travel and the thump, thump, thump of uneven pavement passing right below our feet, not to mention the cigarette smoke and carbon monoxide that crept in, made me more than just a little carsick. Yet, what I really dreaded was that these trips meant one thing for me: while my father spent time with his farmer friends, I would hang out with the children of these farmers doing work such as scooping up cow patties into a pickup truck so the whole mess could be sold for fertilizer.

One weekend I was in a particularly foul mood. After a brief argument about wanting to stay home (which I lost), I gave my father the silent treatment all along the New York Thruway, past the Roscoe Diner (where I actually skipped our usual father-son cheeseburger deluxe lunch—in retrospect, blasphemy), and through the serpentine roads that snaked their way through the Catskill Mountains. My father, generally a quiet man who was known for his quick wit and even quicker temper, took it mostly in stride that day. I, however, was, plain and simple, being a brat. As I looked out the van window at the passing landscape— resentful, hungry, and nauseated—all I wanted to do was barf.

As we pulled into the dirt driveway of my father's friend's place early that afternoon, I saw, smelled, and experienced something that has stayed with me my entire life. There, about a hundred feet from the house, was a giant pile of muddy cow dung. Through my open window the heap smelled horrendous. My body tightened. I knew that my entire weekend would be spent shoveling this ghastly muck into somebody's pickup truck.

I whispered to myself, "Oh, God, get me out of here."

As if it was an answer to a prayer, God, in a way, did.

As the van came to a stop and I eyed this enormous mound of cow manure, I spotted a bright pink flower growing out of the muck.

One bright pink flower.

Something moved inside me—and the movement occurred not in my stomach but in my heart. For one brief moment I felt something depart from my body. I didn't know then, nor do I know now, exactly what it was. My best guess is that what left me was my bad attitude.

At that point, I laughed. My anger had vanished.

My father studied me as I stared out my window. He leaned on the steering wheel and said, "Holy . . . well, would you look at that."

An off-color story about cow manure may not seem like the best way to open a section on the Stations of the Cross, which is a powerful devotion about suffering, but the point here is that beauty growing from the waste of life is at the very heart of Christianity. Beauty somehow blossoms from all the messes and stinks and repulsive things in the world. In fact, it's what happened to Jesus, who was born into a flawed world, worked among sinners, was betrayed by his friends, and was murdered and left to rot. He became—except to his friends and family—mere human waste.

And yet we know that there is so much more to this story than compost. Something beautiful always is growing from the earth. There is resurrection, there is transformation, and we are privileged to watch reminders of this unending process of death and renewal each and every spring. As above, so below. We should hail each crocus that pushes bravely through the frosty ground as a metaphor for how all the barriers between heaven and earth we think we perceive are just an illusion. We should glean from the example of nature the glorious promise of everlasting life.

The Stations of the Cross is in one regard an examination of suffering. It is also an exercise in being hopeful. Praying the stations offers us a way of walking metaphorically in Jesus's footsteps. To walk through the stations is an examination, a journey of the soul, an exercise in being a witness, a supporter, and a bearer of burdens.

In the Christian tradition, the stations, also known as the Way of the Cross, form a sacred devotion that focuses on the Passion of Christ. Traditionally composed of fourteen events that trace the final path of Jesus's life, from the hours after the Last Supper up until the Crucifixion, the Stations of the Cross is a contemplative, meditative practice. It is a mystical pilgrimage into the suffering heart of Christ. It contains, at its core, the essence of the story of Easter, which has at its center the story of a new exodus, a Moses-like movement out of myopic spiritual slavery into a panoramic promised land of love. These stations are a meditative exercise that has been around since before the Middle Ages, though it was popularized by the Franciscans in the thirteenth and fourteenth centuries. The purpose of the exercise is to make a spiritual pilgrimage through what is arguably the most dramatic moment of Christ's life.

By their very nature, the Stations of the Cross and the images associated with them are emotionally charged. They aren't words printed on a page. They are images; therefore, the impact upon us is, generally speaking, more emotional than intellectual. The stations reveal the lowest point in Jesus's life. Precisely because of this, they resonate with our experiences of difficult times in our lives. They also echo the tough times that we hold in our memories. In these ways, the stations appeal more to the heart than they do to the head. When we take Jesus's suffering into us and ponder *in our hearts* the events he experienced, we are stirred from spiritual sleepwalking. To be awakened like this can be disruptive, perhaps even alarming. But the point of the exercise is to nudge us into thinking about, as Christians who are supposed to be living in imitation of Christ's life, what the stations indicate about where we are on our own faith journey.

One of my favorite poems is Wallace Stevens's "Thirteen Ways of Looking at a Blackbird," which is essentially thirteen very short poems, each one revealing a different side of a blackbird. One afternoon a couple of years ago, I was praying with the Stations of the Cross and I started to see that, like the sections of Stevens's poem that show different aspects of a bird, the various stations offer unique ways to see, understand, and appreciate how Jesus responded to suffering.

What is so remarkable about the Passion is that this is where we find Jesus at his most human. Once Jesus is condemned by the Sanhedrin, there are no miracles. There's no changing water to wine or walking on water. There are no healings. The blind people listening to the commotion in the streets as Jesus is being led to his death do not regain their sight—tellingly, no one even asks to receive his lost sight. This is Jesus bare to the bone. Yet, even in this most corporeal and atrocious of experiences, he doesn't do what most humans might do. He does not behave in typically human ways. No one would have blamed him for cursing his tormenters. And yet he did not. He forgave them. He could have freaked out, ranting and raving against his captors when he was taken and restrained, but he didn't. He stayed calm. Scorn to the point of hatred for Peter, who denied him in his moment of need, would have been justified. And yet Jesus accepted Peter's weakness and then, astonishingly, still wanted Peter to be the rock of the Church.

Yet, I struggled with the stations for most of my life. I spent twelve years in Catholic school; praying the Stations of the Cross was something my classmates and I did every year. However, I never really connected with the stations, and as I moved into adulthood I still didn't feel a connection. I preferred Christmas for the celebratory happiness it brings. What changed my view of the stations was the life-altering experience of saying good-bye to someone I loved with all my heart.

A few years ago, I was alone in a hospital room with my grandmother, who was dying. She had been like a second mom to me, so seeing her hooked up to monitors and watching her struggle to breathe cut me to the quick and made me feel helpless. I was holding her hand in mine. All of a sudden, I felt as if I had actually experienced all the pain she had suffered in her life. It was as though her sufferings were transmitted to me via our joined hands. Although the experience was fleeting, it left a profound mark upon me. Sometime after my grandmother passed away, I felt drawn to the stations and began to meditate and pray with them all throughout the year (I don't know why; I wasn't thinking about it). Now, a few years later, each station is, for me, a reminder to live with integrity. I may fall short of this personal goal, but as the Stations of the Cross and the Resurrection reveal, God is always there to lift me up whenever I do fall.

Monday through Friday I ride the Long Island Rail Road from

my home in Rockville Centre to my job in Midtown Manhattan. Often I take the express train, which zips me into the city rather quickly. After work, however, I have to take the local, which incorporates numerous station stops along the way. What this means for me is that it takes a lot longer to get home than it does to get to work. This is particularly not fun when I'm packed in with dozens of tired, grumpy, sometimes smelly passengers, all of whom only want one thing: to get home.

I hate taking the local, but over the years I've come to see that this particular train forces me to slow down after having been on the go all day. Though I usually bury my nose in a book, recently I have started paying more attention to stations and stops along the way. There's the Forest Hills station, where tree-lined streets and delicate brickwork make me feel like I'm pulling into a Tudor garden. Then there's the more urban Kew Gardens station. The station for this bustling, noisy, crowded area of Queens sports a modest platform that is raised only about three feet above the ground. My point here is that over the years I have come to see that each station has its own characteristics and personality. Each is a point of arrival and departure for people just like me, all of whom are doing various things to fulfill their specific responsibilities to themselves and others. Each of these stations tells a complex story.

Of course, you know where I'm going here. Traveling by public transportation is not that different from journeying through the Stations of the Cross. Both require that I slow down and, if I'm smart, pay attention. I know I've been guilty of zipping through the stories in the Gospels—there's Christmas (presents!) and then bam, we're into Easter (chocolate bunnies!). But, the Stations say, *Slow down. Pay particular attention to these specific moments in Jesus's life.* Just like the stations on the Babylon branch of the Long Island

Rail Road, each of the Stations of the Cross has its own tales to tell and lessons to be learned. For instance, consider the particular station in which Veronica wipes the face of Jesus. It's a visually dramatic moment that demonstrates how active compassion imparts a gift. For Veronica, it was the image of Christ's face upon her cloth. For us, it's the image of Jesus's smile imprinted on our hearts.

In the past year I've wanted to get to know Jesus more deeply, and I've been able to accomplish this by focusing on the trials he experienced at the end of his life. So I began applying a variation of the Examen to the Stations of the Cross during my evening commute. I make it a fifteen-day exercise (I add the Resurrection to the fourteen stations), focusing on just one station a day, Monday through Friday, which makes for a three-week exercise (call it my own personal novena). This structured schedule of praying has helped me decompress at the same time as it has helped me develop my relationship with Jesus in new ways. On those days when my head is still with my work, an alarm set on my phone ensures that I won't forget my intention.

I invite you to find a way to incorporate this reflection into your life. There is no wrong time to pray. You can pray the Stations of the Cross before or after work, before or after taking your children to school, or if you are retired or work from home, perhaps you could pray the Stations as you drink your morning cup of coffee or tea.

Here are five simple steps, derived from the Examen, to help you unlock the Stations and make them an integral part of your spiritual life in a practical, contemplative, and reflective way.

Step 1: Choose a Station. Let's say we're focusing on Jesus taking up his cross. You can read a passage from the Bible that correlates to that scene or simply picture an image in your mind. Then take a few deep breaths and ask God to help you quiet your head and open your heart. Often we try to focus only on getting rid of all the mental chatter inside us, but it's also important to place your attention on the waves of emotion and feelings inside you. Something in you might resist focusing. You may feel tired, nervous, or angry on any given day, but that's okay. Be forgiving of yourself. Just allow yourself to find a level of openness that is authentic in that moment.

Step 2: Remind yourself that God is all around you. He's inside you and outside you. His mind is present in your mind and his heart beats in yours. Try to feel that reality as best as you can. Then conjure forth the image of Jesus carrying his cross and bring it inside. Using your imagination, place that image inside you. Let it take root in you. Let it rest there.

Step 3: Ask the Holy Spirit to rise up inside you and give you the wisdom to acknowledge God in your life. Ask the Spirit to help you meditate on the scene inside you. How do you think Jesus felt when this was happening? What was he thinking? What is your cross to bear? How heavy is it? How does it affect your relationship with God?

Step 4: Review your day. Where did your cross feel the heaviest today? Where did you encounter the cross on the shoulders of others at work, on the news, or in the streets? Where is God in these encounters? Ask him to make you more aware of and compassionate toward others and yourself. Did you make an effort to see someone else's cross? What did you do to help that person carry his or her burden?

Step 5: Give thanks to God for the opportunity to know Jesus better and ask God to help you become more aware of the crosses that everyone carries in life.

The First Station: Jesus Is Condemned to Death

"Now at the festival the governor was accustomed to release a prisoner for the crowd, anyone whom they wanted. At that time they had a notorious prisoner called Jesus Barabbas. So after they had gathered, Pilate said to them, 'Whom do you want me to release for you, Jesus Barabbas or Jesus who is called the Messiah?' For he realized that it was out of jealousy that they had handed him over. While he was sitting on the judgment seat, his wife sent word to him, 'Have nothing to do with that innocent man, for today I have suffered a great deal because of a dream about him.' Now the chief priests and the elders persuaded the crowds to ask for Barabbas and to have Jesus killed. The governor again said to them, 'Which of the two do you want me to release for you?' And they said, 'Barabbas.' Pilate said to them, 'Then what should I do with Jesus who is called the Messiah?' All of them said, 'Let him be crucified!'" (Matthew 27:15–22)

REFLECT

♦ Imagine that you are one of the people in the crowd. What do you feel as you witness Christ being judged this way?

- When in your life have you followed the crowd instead of following the inner voice that is God?
- How can you help your children and other young people recognize crowd mentality for the bullying it is, and then react in ways that mitigate suffering and injustice?
- Contemplate the aftereffects of this kind of scenario. Putting yourself in the shoes of the scourged as well as those doing the scourging is worthy of meditative time.

The Second Station: Jesus Carries His Cross

"Then the soldiers of the governor took Jesus into the governor's headquarters, and they gathered the whole cohort around him. They stripped him and put a scarlet robe on him, and after twisting some thorns into a crown, they put it on his head. They put a reed in his right hand and knelt before him and mocked him, saying, 'Hail, King of the Jews!' They spat on him, and took the reed and struck him on the head. After mocking him, they stripped him of the robe and put his own clothes on him. Then they led him away to crucify him." (Matthew 27:27–31)

REFLECT

- Imagine that you are Christ as he's mocked and abused by Roman soldiers. Imagine the pain he must have suffered and the humiliation he must have felt at the hands of these people. Imagine the blows. Imagine the spit on his face. Imagine being struck in the head repeatedly.
- What do you see? How do you feel? How do you respond?
- Have you ever witnessed someone being bullied in this way? Have you yourself been bullied or physically abused?

Consider that Jesus wants you to know that he understands your pain because he too suffered in this way. Does having this in common with him give you solace?

♦ Think about what you can do to help others who are victims of public humiliation and/or physical abuse.

The Third Station: Jesus Falls for the First Time

How long, O Lord? Will you forget me forever?
How long will you hide your face from me?
How long must I bear pain in my soul,
and have sorrow in my heart all day long?
How long shall my enemy be exalted over me?

Consider and answer me, O Lord my God!
Give light to my eyes, or I will sleep the sleep of death,
and my enemy will say, "I have prevailed";
my foes will rejoice because I am shaken.

But I trusted in your steadfast love;
my heart shall rejoice in your salvation.
I will sing to the Lord
because he has dealt bountifully with me.

(PSALM 13:1–6)

REFLECT

♦ Imagine watching Christ fall, weakened beyond his human strength. Have you ever suffered this kind of collapse from illness or injury? What was your reaction? What strategies did you employ to maintain your dignity?

♦ Imagine how difficult it was for God to watch the struggles of his beloved son. Have you ever witnessed a loved one going through challenges so complete that a mental, physical, or emotional collapse was suffered as a result? If so, what was your reaction? How did you handle their moment of need?

♦ Ask yourself: How can I help when similar situations arise? In other words, how can I partner with God to help alleviate the burdens of others?

♦ Have you ever felt as if God abandoned you? How did that make you feel? How did it affect your faith? Did your faith waver or grow stronger through these experiences? How can you use this experience to assist others when they are spiritually challenged?

♦ What does this Station say about love? Where can you find love in this Station? Perhaps it is in the pain the observer suffers in his or her own heart. To allow people to travel their own painful journey while one stands close by in support is sometimes as painful as traveling such a journey oneself. For example, as a parent, you would gladly trade perfect health for the cancer with which your child has been diagnosed, and yet you cannot. What does this Station tell us about the value of standing as witness, even though it is painful to do so, to dignify the sufferings of our loved ones?

The Fourth Station: Jesus Meets His Mother

"Then Simeon blessed them and said to his mother Mary, 'This child is destined for the falling and the rising of many in Israel, and to be a sign that will be opposed so that the inner thoughts of many will be revealed—and a sword will pierce your own soul too.'" (Luke 2:34–35)

REFLECT

- Imagine you are the mother of Christ. What do you feel as you watch this scene in which your grown son's suffering unfolds in front of you?

- What do you want to do? Are you angry with God for allowing this to happen? Do you expect him to rescue your son? Do you plead with him to intercede or do you accept what appears to be God's will?

- Have you ever been helpless in the face of your child's suffering? Have you endured the agony of not being able to help when your child is in danger? If not, consider those mothers who have. Imagine for a moment the mother who has never lived in anything but poverty as she shuffles into a grandiose courtroom where strangers will decide the fate of her child. Imagine a different mother, one whose child died when a drunk driver smashed into the family car. Consider how much helplessness is built into our criminal justice system. Consider what can be done to correct the systemic miscarriage of justice.

- If you have endured a similar horror in which you were forced to stand by helplessly, unable to stop something horribly wrong from happening to your child, how can you use the stations to comfort and sustain yourself and your child? How can you use the example of the relationship between Jesus and his mother to help your child heal?

The Fifth Station: Simon of Cyrene Helps Carry the Cross

"As they led him away, they seized a man, Simon of Cyrene, who was coming from the country, and they laid the cross on him, and made him carry it behind Jesus. A great number of the people followed him, and among them were women who were beating their breasts and wailing for him." (Luke 23:26–27)

REFLECT

✦ Imagine that you are the bystander, Simon. What do you experience as you watch this man Jesus walk to his death? What does the condemned man look like—what do you see in him? Do you have the courage to look him square in the eyes or is it impossible to meet his gaze? What do you feel for him? Do you feel sorrow? Compassion? Do you feel culpable? Do you wish you could help? Do you welcome the opportunity to help and consider it an honor and a blessing? Does it matter to you how heavy the cross is that you are ordered to carry on his behalf? Do you even feel the weight of the cross or does grace permit you to float above it?

✦ When have you helped someone carry a burden? How did you help? How did this change your life? Did you resent the request to help as an intrusion on your time? Or did you welcome it as a chance to prove your love for God?

Are there people in your life now who need assistance carrying their crosses? How can you help them?

♦ Do you keep your heart attuned to moments of grace? Are you aware and appreciative of the little miracles in life that enable you to endure seemingly impossible travails? Do you give credit to those (both seen and unseen, earthly and heavenly) who give you an assist? Do you thank them? Do you cultivate an appreciative heart?

The Sixth Station: Veronica Wipes the Face of Jesus
"Restore us, O God; let your face shine, that we may be saved." (Psalm 80:3)

REFLECT

♦ Imagine that you are looking into the eyes of Christ. First of all, can you? Or do you shrink from the fathomlessness in his eyes? Have you ever looked into the face of someone who has seen you at your worst? Is it courage or grace that allows you to face the ugliness you see mirrored in his or her eyes? Contemplate the fact that you will, in fact, stand before Jesus at the end of your life. Will you be able to look into his eyes? Why or why not? How can you use the contemplation of this moment to dictate the way you choose to live?

♦ Have you ever seen the face of Christ in another? If so, what did you experience on an emotional level at that moment? Did the experience affect your faith, and if so, in what way? Does that seminal moment come back to you, as does the moment when I felt my grandmother's

life coursing from her hand through mine, as a reminder
of the opportunities you should be seeking and the moments you should be valuing?

The Seventh Station: Jesus Falls the Second Time

Our steps are made firm by the Lord,
when he delights in our way;
though we stumble, we shall not fall headlong,
for the Lord holds us by the hand.

(PSALM 37:23–24)

REFLECT

♦ When have you stumbled in your life? When have you
stumbled in your faith? Did you feel the hand of God trying to help you up? Did you reach out to ask for his helping hand? Did you accept or refuse his proffered hand?

♦ Memorize this psalm and use it as a prayer when you are
struggling with a relationship, a job, a memory, or an illness.

♦ Stop for a moment and thank God for your hands. Hands
are essential to our human experience. They are the
agents of creative expression. They are the tools of healing. They are the point of transference when we connect
with living creatures. Do we honor our hands? Do we
show our gratitude for their magnificence by coaxing
from them the very finest contributions we are able to
add to the universe? Will we be proud of what our hands

have wrought when we come to the end of our lives? If the answer here is anything but yes, contemplate how you can make a U-turn at this very moment so that you can change how you use your hands. What steps will you need to take to get from here to there—from, for example, hitting to healing?

The Eighth Station: Jesus Meets the Women of Jerusalem

"But Jesus turned to them and said, 'Daughters of Jerusalem, do not weep for me, but weep for yourselves and for your children. For the days are surely coming when they will say, "Blessed are the barren, and the wombs that never bore, and the breasts that never nursed." Then they will begin to say to the mountains, "Fall on us"; and to the hills, "Cover us." For if they do this when the wood is green, what will happen when it is dry?'" (Luke 23:28–31)

REFLECT

◆ These are strong words from Christ. What do they mean to you? Do they reflect how you feel about your own place in society? Do you recoil from the ominous dread that seemingly blankets the world? Do you fear that the growth of evil is unstoppable, and that whatever efforts you make are puny and ineffective in the face of such pervasive doom? What does Jesus's completion of his terrible journey show us about how we approach the inevitable? Do we give up? Or do we confront and carry out our personal destinies with courage, dignity, and faith?

◆ Do you feel that we are in a green or a dry period in history? Consider this question from a metaphorical point of view: Are you in a green or a dry period of your life? How can you irrigate a barren inner landscape? If things are going well for you, what can you do to prepare for the not-so-good times that are "surely coming"?

♦ How can you, with the power of the Holy Spirit, help transform universal cries of suffering into shouts of jubilation? Do you start small and work to enlarge the size of the canvas on which you are painting the picture of your life's work? Or do you tackle something big, trusting that your work will eventually expose you to the individuals who make up this choir of voices singing a requiem for our world? Or will you stand back like a wallflower at the dance, a bystander to the Passion, an observer too frightened or insecure to risk becoming involved? Consider the consequences of your choice, whichever it may be.

The Ninth Station: Jesus Falls the Third Time

The Lord upholds all who are falling,
and raises up all who are bowed down.

(PSALM 145:14)

REFLECT

♦ When have you fallen, and how has God raised you up?

♦ By nature, are you a glass-half-full or glass-half-empty person? Consider how optimism parallels Christ's journey. Brainstorm reflexive reactions you can practice that incorporate an optimistic approach to the challenges life presents.

♦ How can you raise God up in the course of your ordinary life?

The Tenth Station: Jesus Is Stripped of His Garments

"When the soldiers had crucified Jesus, they took his clothes and divided them into four parts, one for each soldier. They also took his tunic; now the tunic was seamless, woven in one piece from the top. So they said to one another, 'Let us not tear it, but cast lots for it to see who will get it.' This was to fulfill what the scripture says, 'They divided my clothes among themselves, and for my clothing they cast lots.'" (John 19:23–24)

REFLECT

♦ What is the significance of the seamless garment? How can we do a better job of clothing ourselves seamlessly with Christ's example? How can we become more comfortable "wearing" Christ in our own personalities, characters, and actions?

♦ In what ways do we strip God from our lives?

The Eleventh Station: Jesus Is Nailed to the Cross

"Then they brought Jesus to the place called Golgotha (which means the place of the skull). And they offered him wine mixed with myrrh; but he did not take it. . . . And with him they crucified two bandits, one on his right and one on his left. Those who passed by derided him, shaking their heads and saying, 'Aha!

You who would destroy the temple and build it in three days, save yourself, and come down from the cross!' " (Mark 15:22–23, 27–30)

REFLECT

♦ Imagine that you are Christ dying on the cross. What do you feel? What is going through your mind?

♦ In what ways do we crucify God day by day? In what ways do we crucify one another?

♦ Where and how do "little crucifixions" of people and animals occur in contemporary society, and what role do we play in their perpetuation? Are we uninvolved bystanders, active participants, those who crucify, or those who intervene to halt the cruelty? What changes can you make in your life right now that will better align yourself with Christ's message of peace?

The Twelfth Station: Jesus Dies on the Cross

"When it was noon, darkness came over the whole land until three in the afternoon. At three o'clock Jesus cried out with a loud voice, 'Eloi, Eloi, lema sabachthani?' which means, 'My God, my God, why have you forsaken me?' When some of the bystanders heard it, they said, 'Listen, he is calling for Elijah.' And someone ran, filled a sponge with sour wine, put it on a stick, and gave it to him to drink, saying, 'Wait, let us see whether Elijah will come to take him down.' Then Jesus gave a loud cry and breathed his last." (Mark 15:33–37)

REFLECT

◆ Why does Christ call out, "My God, my God, why have you forsaken me"? Do you think he believed that his Father had abandoned him?

◆ Have you ever felt that God has abandoned you? Is this feeling rooted in the experience of having been abandoned by someone in your life? Or do you carry the guilt of having abandoned someone—family, friend, coworker, or stranger—who was counting on you? If so, what can you do now to make it right and promote healing and growth?

The Thirteenth Station: Jesus Is Taken Down from the Cross
"Joseph of Arimathea, a respected member of the council, who was also himself waiting expectantly for the kingdom of God, went boldly to Pilate and asked for the body of Jesus. Then Pilate wondered if he were already dead; and summoning the centurion, he asked him whether he had been dead for some time. When he learned from the centurion that he was dead, he granted the body to Joseph." (Mark 15:43–45)

REFLECT

◆ How can you, here and now, carry the body of Christ?

◆ Do you cultivate an active awareness of your responsibility as a member of the body of Christ?

◆ Looking at the wounds of Christ as symbolic of all the hurt and suffering in the universe, do you make everyday decisions based on an awareness of God's reliance on you, a member of the body of Christ, to help heal his wounded world?

The Fourteenth Station: Jesus Is Buried in the Tomb

"Then Joseph bought a linen cloth, and taking down the body, wrapped it in the linen cloth, and laid it in a tomb that had been hewn out of the rock. He then rolled a stone against the door of the tomb. Mary Magdalene and Mary the mother of Joses saw where the body was laid." (Mark 15:46–47)

REFLECT

♦ Imagine that you are walking with Mary Magdalene, Mary, and Joseph of Arimathea. What do you feel as you stand before the tomb?

♦ How can we emulate their example in real life? Do you take seriously the biblical admonition to help bury the dead? Are you there emotionally and physically to support and sustain friends and family when someone they love has died?

The Fifteenth Station: The Resurrection

"After the Sabbath, as the first day of the week was dawning, Mary Magdalene and the other Mary went to see the tomb. And suddenly there was a great earthquake; for an angel of the Lord, descending from heaven, came and rolled back the stone and sat on it. His appearance was like lightning, and his clothing white as snow. For fear of him the guards shook and became like dead men. But the angel said to the women, 'Do not be afraid; I know that you are looking for Jesus who was crucified. He is not here; for he has been raised, as he said. Come, see the place where he lay. Then go quickly and tell his disciples, "He has been raised from the dead, and indeed he is going ahead of you to Galilee; there you will see him." This is my message for you.'" (Matthew 28:1–7)

REFLECT

- ◆ Imagine you are with Mary Magdalene as she looks in the tomb. Imagine you see a figure in white telling you that Christ has risen from the dead. What does this mean to you? What do you feel? What is the expression on Mary's face? Are you filled with happiness? Disbelief?
- ◆ What is the significance of the Resurrection to your life?
- ◆ How can you bring the message of hope and redemption signified by Christ's resurrection to those who are poor, homeless, incarcerated, agnostic?

CHAPTER 15

Reality

Consciousness cannot be accounted for in physical terms.
For consciousness is absolutely fundamental. It cannot be
accounted for in terms of anything else.

—ERWIN SCHRÖDINGER

As an editor I've been fortunate enough over the years to work with a number of scientists, medical doctors, and researchers who all believe that consciousness determines reality. What does this mean? Dozens and dozens of books have been written to try to unpack that idea, but on a basic level I think it simply means that our awareness determines the life we lead; our outlook as well as our in-look creates the world around us. As someone who spent twelve years in Catholic school, has spent countless hours in prayer, and has attended hundreds of church services, I have a very Catholic awareness of the world. Unlike for many of my agnostic and atheist brothers and sisters, God, Jesus, Mary, and the saints are an everyday reality for me. These spiritual realities, I think it is safe to say, are not a personal reality to nonbelievers, who may have had very little interaction with Catholic thinking and may have no use for Jesus in their lives. This does not mean that nonbelievers are bad people or that Jesus doesn't exist and isn't God, just that these people have never had the types of encounters that I and millions of others have had.

Think of it like this: Suppose you and your friend are attending a holiday party where none of the people in attendance have ever met your pal. Your friend exists, is very real. But your colleagues have never had an encounter with this particular person until you introduce him or her to them. To those people you work with, your friend was a non-reality, a mere name, perhaps a face in a picture. But after the encounter, what was unreal—or as quantum physicists might say, was just a potentiality—becomes reality.

A book is very different from a party, but my musings here have been my attempt to introduce you to some of my best friends. They may have been complete strangers to you, or you may have met them before, or you may even hang out with them more than I do. But my experiences and your experiences are unique, and I hope that by sharing my insights about God, Jesus, Mary, the saints, and the angels I have helped you to encounter the real but often unseen realities around us in new ways.

For a moment I want to come back to this idea that consciousness determines reality. Jesus was not a quantum physicist, but he believed and taught that the measure of our faith and belief determines our relationship with God. In the Gospel of Mark, Jesus says, "So I tell you, whatever you ask for in prayer, *believe* that you have received it, and it will be yours" (11:24; emphasis added). Jesus isn't pulling any punches. He's saying that the outcomes of life are based on what we believe as well as the degree to which we believe that something is so. If we believe God is a vengeful God, he will probably be a vengeful God, not because he is vengeful, but because we see the world through vengeful eyes. If we believe Jesus is a fraud, then we'll be able to find two thousand years of bad behavior from Christians around the world that seems to back this idea up. Does this mean that Jesus is a fraud? No. But we bring our own beliefs to a reality that in turn becomes a personal reality for us. Do we believe that Jesus meant it when he said, "Anyone who believes in me will do the same works I have done, and even greater works" (John 14:12)? In other words, if we believe that we too can be miracle workers, healers, and prophets, we will be able to do these things and more. That is a serious statement. Imagine what our world would be like if we actually lived every day believing this fully.

Jesus knows that we human beings are thickheaded. When he was physically present on earth he performed extraordinary healings (curing leprosy with a touch of his hand and restoring sight to the blind) and feats that contradict what we know about physics (walking on water, calming the weather). Why? To show off? To take advantage of people? No. He performed miracles to highlight God's glory and power in the world. To shine the spotlight on life everlasting. Cynics will say that the writers of these stories just made them up, that they are embellishments of the imagination, that there can be no virgin birth—it's physically impossible—that someone can't be dead for three days and come back to life. These people deny the miraculous. Why? For many reasons, but chief among them is that they may never have had an experience of the miraculous; hence, they determine that miracles do not exist. It would be like me describing a car to someone who lived in the Australian outback, someone who has never had contact with what we call the modern world. There are a couple of problems in translation here. One, I probably can't speak the person's language and he or she can't speak mine, so we are already at odds. Two, whatever explanation I provide would probably be doubted until this person could actually experience a car, touch the cool metal, listen to the revving of the engine, smell the gas and the leather seats, and finally ride in it with the windows open. Hence, experience determines our personal reality.

Belief helps to activate the reality of God in our lives. This doesn't mean that I create God with my belief. He and the miraculous exist regardless of my belief, just as a long-lost uncle might exist even if we've never seen each other. But we can live a miraculous life if we *believe* we can live a miraculous life. Awareness determines our reality, our faith determines our reality, and our beliefs determine our reality. If we believe we are spiritually homeless, we are going to feel alone. Our beliefs determine how we experience life, but a shifting of consciousness can collapse the walls of our limitations and reveal that we are living in a house with a loving extended family waiting for us to come to dinner. Devotions and prayers are a way of shifting our consciousness.

Now, I don't want to put the full onus on us. We live in the twenty-first century, which means that there are two thousand years of Christian history, theology, celebrations, mistakes, falsehoods, and heresies that influence the way we see our faith. Take the miracles of the saints, for instance. Over the years many have reported that saints have levitated, been in two places at one time, healed the sick, resurrected the dead, and even manifested the wounds of Jesus in the stigmata (St. Francis may have done all of these things). Yet, knowing about these extraordinary events can have the effect of making us blind to simple, everyday miracles. I think it would do all of us a world of good if we looked at miracles from an Old Testament point of view. In the Jewish tradition at the time when Jesus lived, a miracle was a sign of God's presence in our lives. *A sign.* Back then there wasn't a separation of the world into faith and reason, science and God. Everything came from God. Miracles of varying degrees happened every day. The entire world in which the Hebrews lived was infused with God. A miracle could be the parting of the Red Sea, an exorcism, the touch of the wind on one's face, a communal meal, or a cup of water shared with a friend. If we want the miraculous to appear in our lives, then it might help if we looked for small signs of God in our lives. As St. Ignatius said, "Seek God in all things." We can look for God in the food we eat, in our work, in our sickness, in our celebrations, our relationships, our brokenness, our doubts, our weariness, our worries, and our wanderings. When we do, the miraculous blossoms before our eyes, our prayers are answered, and we experience not necessarily something extraordinary, but a heightened sense of the ordinary.

Experiencing life everlasting, experiencing God in the here and now, involves commitment. There's no way around this. Often we are afraid to commit to God. I know I have been guilty of this in the past. Growing up, I didn't want to look foolish around my friends and so my prayers used to be halfhearted. In truth, I can also be extremely lazy. Moreover, I dreaded being disappointed. I didn't want to ask God for something and not get it, so my devotion was lukewarm. Who wants lukewarm food? Even God would spit lukewarm out of his mouth. No, we want hot food—though not so hot it burns our tongues and prevents us from tasting anything for the rest of the day. Few of us want cold food (unless it's pizza after a hangover, or vichyssoise at a fancy restaurant). Sure, it can sustain us, but does it excite us? Do we enjoy it? God wants us to appreciate, to revel in our day-to-day lives, to experience wonder and excitement, to be healed, to be forgiven, and ultimately to feel at home, to hang out in a holy house where instead of fifty-inch TVs we have mountains and trees, cityscapes, and people to gaze at with awe.

Before I end this book, I want to leave you with one final story.

CHAPTER 16

St. Cecelia: A Vision and a Sort of Homecoming

(for Anthony DeStefano)

We are told that you heard angels sing.
—FROM A PRAYER TO ST. CECELIA

It is 2014 and I am in Rome on business. I am sitting at an outside table at the Ristorante Sette Oche in Altalena in Trastevere, beneath a white canopy, eating my dinner alone. The people at the table next to me—a middle-aged couple in T-shirts—are talking about as much as I am. When they do speak it's in German. I can't understand what they are saying, but there is no laughter, not a single smile. Still, I love them. I am in love with so many tonight—with my family back home, these strangers, the streets of brick and cobblestone, the facades of buildings with their chiseled angels and saints and gargoyles looking down upon me. A breeze blowing in from the alleyway touches all of us in unison, weaving us together for a once-in-a-lifetime event now. I will never see these people again. Most will not know the sound of my voice and I will not know their pain or lost desires, but I will carry something of them wherever I go—like the memory of the small bump on the cheek of an old woman eating pineapple and drinking coffee just a few tables away.

I have ordered chicken and prosciutto mixed with penne and Gorgonzola. When it arrives the meal looks dry. The salad is dry too—a few lettuce leaves, a hiccup of radicchio, nothing else. None of it looks appetizing. Yet after the first bite I realize, like so many other times in my life, looks can be deceiving. The food is delicious, and my mouth blooms with a perfect combination of meat, pasta, salt, pepper, olive oil, and cheese. Near perfection can be found in simple things like this as well as in the way a man across from me pinches his nose when he laughs, seated with his teenage son and drinking beer as the bare-shouldered girl next to them moves her pizza around her plate. The son checks his phone. His father sneezes. Gray hair curls at the base of the older man's neck. He laughs again. He pinches his nose. His son smiles and checks his phone again. No sneeze. The girl takes a bite.

I finish the chicken and wash it down with beer. The beer tastes cold as it goes down and I think that might be a line from *The Sun Also Rises*. Hemingway was always washing down his food with cold beer, and then the cold would turn warm and he would drink another to cool down again, and he would keep drinking until a memory no longer felt like a boxer's punch to the face. All of this happened as rain fell.

There is no rain tonight. I can see a glimpse of sky, crepuscular and blue like jazz. I see my waiter approaching. I learned a couple of years ago that when an Italian waiter asks you if you want a cappuccino, he is making fun of you. Stupid Americans love cappuccino. This waiter tonight asks me if I want cappuccino. Ah, I'm on to you, signore! "No, I will have espresso," I say in Italian. The beer was cold; the espresso is warm and it tastes like smoke.

I get the check and walk down the Via della Lungaretta. I see you, St. Cecelia, peeking around a corner. I run to the edge of the building, thick-walled, medieval, yellow, and decorated with flowerpots. I look right. You're not there, but in the distance I see your silhouette against a gilded mosaic wall that is hundreds of years old, but beneath the streetlamps the image shines brightly around you (or is it you that shines brightly around everything?). I give chase but the throat-clearing roar of a Vespa distracts me. Turning, I see an old man wearing a World War I German helmet cruising the Vespa over the cobblestones. When I look back, you're gone. In your place is a woman, a dark angel, a raven in a lace shawl. She stretches out her arms. She moves to the left and I lose sight of her. She vanishes like a prophecy. In the distance, a violin, a flute, and a cello. I follow the sound and it leads me to your church.

O, noble Cecelia, lily of heaven, patron saint of musicians, how you suffered in life, but you bring me friendship tonight. Slabs of broken marble engraved with names long gone from a world I never knew adorn an entrance to your holy home. I walk through the entrance to the church. Faint music rises like incense. I look up and then to my left and the young woman and her family from the restaurant are standing there, her shoulders now covered, showing respect for the invisible, as she leans, arches her back, her face tan, her hair brown and gold, and stares at the ceiling of this church. A choir practices hallelujahs around an altar.

This is where heaven is.

This is life everlasting.

It's in the way an old woman's long gray hair falls along her back as she kneels and prays. It's here, many years away, many miles away, many memories away. It's here, on the many late-night walks with my wife and two sons on a sand-strewn boardwalk in winter. It is here among these voices and these penitents with heads bowed and hearts raised.

We the fallen get lost. Moving from place to place, from thought to thought, sometimes we stop and roll back stones only to find empty tombs. And yet, we sense something. Something. It runs through us like a swallowed needle, cutting us all the way down, creating wounds we cannot see. Angels and saints, sons and fathers, ghosts and mothers move through our hearts. We feel them in the muscles of our arms, the softness of our bellies, and the way a whisper enters our ears.

We believe in all that is seen and unseen. It's all the same.

St. Cecelia, I feel your presence all over. There is so much I want to tell you! I have seen life everlasting in the sound of an organ in a cathedral. I have tasted heaven in the way you look upon things. I have heard the trumpets of eternal life in my children's footfalls on creaky staircases. This is what it means. Look no further. It is here and now in the cold our hands feel as they touch the marble. It is in our coughs and in the pain in our feet.

Take a breath now. Hold it. Hold life everlasting in your mouth, touch it with your tongue, grind it with your teeth. Know it presses against you as you press against it.

You want proof of heaven? It's in the taste of salt. In an argument. In fingers that touch. In sunrises and moonsets. In the silence of a candle's flame.

I look up. A fresco of a Madonna and child. I say a prayer and turn to leave and see a mother nursing her child in a chair against a gray wall. Her skin is so white. The baby is pressed against her, its head in her hand. I smile at her and she smiles back. Now is here. Living paint on fresh plaster.

Outside, shadows fall on an obelisk. St. Cecelia walks with me, her spirit a hieroglyph, pointing to something I don't fully understand. This unknown something calls to me and I want to fly. I would like to grab hold on the back of an angel and soar above the drunk and lonely who walk up and down these streets tonight.

I am in love with so many tonight, with my wife and my sons back home, with the angels, who refuse to show their faces, and with you, St. Cecelia, you who are beside me one minute and running away and turning corners the next. I even love the fool talking loudly on his cell phone as a choir of human seraphim in polyester and jeans sing night prayers for all of us on the streets of this holy city.

How do we know God? Not by standing strong with puffed-out chests, not with fists, but by dissolving like sugar in coffee, salt in a pot of water, his body into hers, her body into his.

Remember, St. Cecelia says, you know an angel when its wings cast no shadow. All others are impostors.

Remember.

A bell rings and something vibrates through me and then fades.

"Cast no shadows where you tread," St. Cecelia whispers to me.

"I want to go home," I say to myself.

Then like a breath in my ear, a still, small voice, not the saint's, says, "Yes, but you are home with me always."

God the Father, pray for us.
Jesus the Son, pray for us.
Holy Spirit, pray for us.
Mother Mary, pray for us.
Angels with shadowless wings, pray for us.
St. Cecelia, pray for us.

APPENDIX I

Spiritual 911

What do you do if you find yourself stranded on the side of the road with a flat tire and your jack isn't working correctly? What if your child is in the emergency room or your aunt shows up at your door late at night drunk and about to pass out? What do you do if your mother is suffering from mental illness and she's having a meltdown in front of your kids? Well, try to get physical help. Call a tow truck, the police, a doctor, a therapist, or a priest. But also, pray.

What follows is a toolbox of prayers that we can use when we're in a precarious situation and in need of immediate spiritual assistance. We start with the basics such as the Our Father and Hail Mary, always a good idea when we're under pressure. But we can always appeal to the saints to help us as well. Think of them as your soul's personal EMTs, who, since they've also lived through difficult times, can help us when we are experiencing an emergency. We can pray with St. Dymphna or St. Gemma Galgani when we have a migraine or our friend is feeling depressed. We can call upon St. Joseph, Jesus's adoptive father, to help when our son or daughter has a dangerous fever. We can ask St. Peregrine to pray with us if we are suffering from illness or get news that a colleague has cancer.

All prayers should ultimately be directed to God, so even

though the saints can serve as advocates and friends, bringing knowledge and assistance to our time of need, keep the Almighty in the forefront of your mind and heart. Our heavenly helpers would want us to do that too.

BASIC PRAYERS

Sign of the Cross

In the name of the Father,
and of the Son,
and of the Holy Spirit.
Amen.

Hail Mary

Hail Mary, full of grace,
the Lord is with you.
Blessed are you among women,
and blessed is the fruit of your womb, Jesus.
Holy Mary, Mother of God,
pray for us sinners,
now and at the hour of our death.
Amen.

Lord's Prayer

Our Father,
who art in heaven,
hallowed be thy name;

thy kingdom come;
thy will be done
on earth as it is in heaven.
Give us this day our daily bread;
and forgive us our trespasses
as we forgive those who trespass against us;
and lead us not into temptation,
but deliver us from evil.
Amen.

Glory Be to the Father (Doxology)

Glory be to the Father,
and to the Son,
and to the Holy Spirit.
As it was in the beginning,
is now, and ever shall be,
world without end.
Amen.

Apostles' Creed

I believe in God,
the Father almighty,
Creator of heaven and earth,
and in Jesus Christ, his only son, our Lord,
who was conceived by the Holy Spirit,
born of the Virgin Mary,
suffered under Pontius Pilate,
was crucified, died, and was buried;

he descended into hell;
on the third day he rose again from the dead;
he ascended into heaven,
and is seated at the right hand of God the Father almighty;
from there he will come to judge the living and the dead.
I believe in the Holy Spirit,
the holy catholic Church,
the communion of saints,
the forgiveness of sins,
the resurrection of the body,
and life everlasting. Amen.

Memorare

Remember, most loving Virgin Mary,
never was it heard
that anyone who turned to you for help
was left unaided.

Inspired by this confidence,
though burdened by my sins,
I run to your protection
for you are my mother.

Mother of the Word of God,
do not despise my words of pleading
but be merciful and hear my prayer.
Amen.

Hail, Holy Queen

Hail, holy Queen, Mother of Mercy,

Our life, our sweetness, and our hope.

To you do we cry,

Poor banished children of Eve;

To you do we send up our sighs,

Mourning and weeping in this valley of tears.

Turn then, most gracious advocate,

Your eyes of mercy toward us;

And after this our exile,

Show us the blessed fruit of your womb, Jesus.

O clement, O loving,

O sweet Virgin Mary.

Pray for us, O holy Mother of God,

that we may be made worthy of the promises of Christ.

PRAYERS FOR DIFFICULT TIMES

Prayer of St. Francis de Sales for Inner Peace
(This is one of my favorite prayers. Whenever fear has a grip on you, or you're experiencing self-doubt, or simply whenever you're in trouble, this prayer brings great comfort.)

Be not afraid. Do not look forward to the changes and chances of this life in fear; rather look to them in full hope that, as they arise, God, whose you are, will deliver you out of them. He has kept you until now, so hold fast to his dear hand and he will lead you safely through all things, and when you cannot stand, he will bear you safely in his arms.

Do not look forward to what may happen tomorrow; the same everlasting Father who cares for you today will take care of you tomorrow and every day. Either he will shield you from suffering or he will give you unfailing strength to bear it.

Be at peace, then, and put away all anxious thought and imaginations.

Prayer of St. Teresa of Ávila for Comfort
During Stressful Times

(This is another prayer that has helped whenever I've felt like the world is too big for me.)

Let nothing disturb you. Let nothing frighten you. All things pass. God does not change. Patience achieves everything. Whoever has God lacks nothing. God alone suffices.

Christ has no body now on earth but yours; no hands but yours; no feet but yours. Yours are the eyes through which the compassion of Christ must look out on the world. Yours are the feet with which he is to go about doing good. Yours are the hands with which he is to bless his people.

Prayer to St. Peregrine for Those Suffering from Cancer or
Serious Illness

O, great St. Peregrine, you have been called "the Mighty," "the Wonder-Worker," because of the numerous miracles which you have obtained from God for those who have had recourse to you.

For so many years you bore in your own flesh this cancerous disease that destroys the very fiber of our being, and you had recourse to the source of all grace when the power of man could do no more. You were favored with the vision of Jesus coming down from his cross to heal your affliction. Ask of God and Our Lady the cure of the sick whom we entrust to you.

[Pause here and state the names of the people you are praying for.]

Aided in this way by your powerful intercession, we shall sing to God, now and for all eternity, a song of gratitude for his great goodness and mercy.

Prayer to St. Dymphna for Mental Healing from Stress, Anxiety, and Nervousness

Lord, our God, you graciously chose St. Dymphna as patroness of those afflicted with mental and nervous disorders and spiritual afflictions. She is thus an inspiration and a symbol of charity to the thousands who ask her intercession.

Please grant, Lord, through the prayers of this pure youthful martyr, relief and consolation to all suffering such trials, and especially those for whom we pray. *[Here mention those for whom you wish to pray.]*

We beg you, Lord, to hear the prayers of St. Dymphna on our behalf. Grant all those for whom we pray patience in their sufferings and resignation to your divine will. Please fill them with hope, and grant them the relief and cure they so much desire.

We ask this through Christ our Lord, who suffered agony in the garden. Amen.

Prayer to St. Expeditus for a Speedy Solution to an Urgent Problem

(St. Expeditus is believed to have been a young Roman solider who was martyred in the fourth century for his faith while serving in

Armenia. He is a much-favored saint in Latin America and can be found on billboards in Brazil. He has also become the patron saint of computer geeks and IT personnel who are in constant need of quick technological solutions.)

St. Expeditus, we humbly beg thee to come to our aid so that thy prompt and certain intercession will obtain for us, from our divine Lord, the grace of a happy and swift solution to the matter which now concerns us. *[Mention your intention.]* We do so without fear, being fully confident in the supreme wisdom of Our Blessed Lord, and place our trust in him without reservation, being mindful that his will alone will be done.

Amen.

Holy Mary, Mother of God, pray for us.

St. Expeditus, our help in urgent matters, pray for us.

(After saying this prayer say three Our Fathers, three Hail Marys, and three Glory Bes.)

Prayer to St. Anthony, Patron of Lost Objects, for Times of Trouble

(Misplaced your wallet? Lost a copy of an old contract? Then St. Anthony is your man. If you're looking to experience a minor miracle, then try this prayer whenever you're in a difficult situation.)

O Holy St. Anthony, gentlest of saints, your love for God and charity for his creatures made you worthy, when on earth, to possess miraculous powers. Encouraged by this thought, I implore you to obtain for me *[your request]*. O gentle and loving St. Anthony, whose heart was ever full of human sympathy, whisper my petition into the ears of the sweet infant Jesus, who loved to be folded in your arms; and the gratitude of my heart will ever be yours. Amen.

Prayer to St. Joseph for Fathers and Families

Oh St. Joseph, whose protection is so great, so strong, so prompt before the throne of God, I place in you all my interests and desires.

Oh St. Joseph, do assist me by your powerful intercession and obtain for me from your divine son all spiritual blessings through Jesus Christ, our Lord, so that having engaged here below your heavenly power I may offer my thanksgiving and homage to the most loving of fathers.

Oh St. Joseph, I never weary contemplating you and Jesus asleep in your arms. I dare not approach while he reposes near your heart. Press him in my name and kiss his fine head for me, and ask him to return the kiss when I draw my dying breath.

St. Joseph, patron of departing souls, pray for us.

Amen.

Prayer to Our Lady of Guadalupe, the Patron Saint of the Americas, for Times of Need, Protection, and for Mothers

Remember, O most gracious Virgin Mary of Guadalupe, that in thy celestial apparitions on the mount of Tepeyac, thou didst promise to show thy compassion and pity toward all who, loving and trusting thee, seek thy help and call upon thee in their necessities and afflictions.

Thou didst promise to hearken to our supplications, to dry our tears, and to give us consolation and relief. Never was it known that anyone who fled to thy protection, implored thy help, or sought thy intercession, either for the common welfare or in personal anxieties, was left unaided.

Inspired with this confidence, we fly unto thee, O Mary, ever Virgin Mother of the true God! Though grieving under the weight of our sins, we come to prostrate ourselves in thy august presence, certain that thou wilt deign to fulfill thy merciful promises. We are full of hope that, standing beneath thy shadow and protection, nothing will trouble or afflict us, nor need we fear illness, or misfortune, or any other sorrow.

Thou hast decided to remain with us through thy admirable image, thou who art our Mother, our health, and our life. Placing ourselves beneath thy maternal gaze and having recourse to thee in all our necessities, we need do nothing more. O Holy Mother of God, despise not our petitions, but in thy mercy hear and answer us.

[Here mention your petition.]

Pray five Hail Marys.

Holy Spirit Prayer of St. Augustine for Times When You Feel Emotionally Lost

(No one really knows if St. Augustine wrote this prayer, but it's been around for hundreds of years. Regardless, it's a beautiful prayer when you are in need of spiritual energy.)

Breathe in me, O Holy Spirit,
That my thoughts may all be holy.
Act in me, O Holy Spirit,
That my work, too, may be holy.
Draw my heart, O Holy Spirit,
That I love but what is holy.
Strengthen me, O Holy Spirit,
To defend all that is holy.
Guard me, then, O Holy Spirit,
That I always may be holy.

The Breastplate of St. Patrick, for Anyone Entering
  into Battle or Facing Challenges
(A popular prayer for soldiers, police officers, and firefighters, this
can be prayed by anyone who is up against difficult odds, whether it
be a court hearing, a difficult talk with a boss, or a stressful meeting.)

I arise today
Through a mighty strength, the invocation of the Trinity,
Through belief in the threeness,
Through confession of the oneness
of the Creator of creation.

I arise today
Through the strength of Christ's birth with his baptism,
Through the strength of his crucifixion with his burial,
Through the strength of his resurrection with his ascension,
Through the strength of his descent for the judgment of
    doom.

I arise today
Through the strength of the love of cherubim,
In the obedience of angels,
In the service of archangels,
In the hope of resurrection to meet with reward,
In the prayers of patriarchs,
In the predictions of prophets,
In the preaching of apostles,
In the faith of confessors,
In the innocence of holy virgins,
In the deeds of righteous men.

I arise today, through
The strength of heaven,
The light of the sun,
The radiance of the moon,
The splendor of fire,
The speed of lightning,
The swiftness of wind,
The depth of the sea,
The stability of the earth,
The firmness of rock.

I arise today, through
God's strength to pilot me,
God's might to uphold me,
God's wisdom to guide me,
God's eye to look before me,
God's ear to hear me,
God's word to speak for me,
God's hand to guard me,
God's shield to protect me,
God's host to save me
From snares of devils,
From temptation of vices,
From everyone who shall wish me ill,
afar and near.

I summon today
All these powers between me and those evils,
Against every cruel and merciless power
that may oppose my body and soul,

Against incantations of false prophets,
Against black laws of pagandom,
Against false laws of heretics,
Against craft of idolatry,
Against spells of witches and smiths and wizards,
Against every knowledge that corrupts man's body and soul;
Christ to shield me today
Against poison, against burning,
Against drowning, against wounding,
So that there may come to me an abundance of reward.

Christ with me,
Christ before me,
Christ behind me,
Christ in me,
Christ beneath me,
Christ above me,
Christ on my right,
Christ on my left,
Christ when I lie down,
Christ when I sit down,
Christ when I arise,
Christ in the heart of every man who thinks of me,
Christ in the mouth of everyone who speaks of me,
Christ in every eye that sees me,
Christ in every ear that hears me.

Prayer to St. Matthew for Help in Financial Situations
(St. Matthew was a tax collector, so he knows something about money. Turn to him when your checking account is dwindling, you're looking for a job, or you have to make a financial decision.)

St. Matthew, as one of Jesus's closest friends, I ask you today to help guide me in all my decisions and endeavors. Please pray with me and intercede on our behalf as we look for assistance in our earthly struggles. Amen.

Prayer to St. Gerard for Expectant Mothers and
*   Those Struggling with Fertility*

St. Gerard,
You worshipped Jesus as the Lord of Life.
I ask you today to pray
For my special intention.
[Mention your intention here.]
Lift up to Jesus
All those who seek to conceive a child,
All those having difficult pregnancies,
All who have suffered the loss of a child,
And all who lovingly lift up their children to God.
Pray that all of us,
By caring for mothers, fathers, and children
born and unborn
May build a culture of life,
In the name of Jesus Christ our Lord. Amen.

Prayer to St. Rita for Impossible Causes like Addiction,
   Financial Troubles, or Anytime You're in Need of a
   Miraculous Turnaround

(In America, St. Jude is venerated as the patron saint of lost causes,
but for centuries Catholics around the world looked to St. Rita to
help them in desperate situations.)

O holy patroness of those in need, St. Rita, whose pleadings
before thy divine Lord are almost irresistible, who for thy lavish-
ness in granting favors hast been called the Advocate of the Hopeless and even of the Impossible; St. Rita, so humble, so pure, so
mortified, so patient, and of such compassionate love for thy crucified Jesus that thou couldst obtain from him whatsoever thou
askest, on account of which all confidently have recourse to thee
expecting, if not always relief, at least comfort; be propitious to
our petition, showing thy power with God on behalf of thy suppli-
ant; be lavish to us, as thou hast been in so many wonderful cases,
for the greater glory of God, for the spreading of thine own devotion, and for the consolation of those who trust in thee.

We promise, if our petition is granted, to glorify thee by making known thy favor, to bless and sing thy praises forever. Relying
then upon thy merits and power before the Sacred Heart of Jesus,
we pray thee grant that *[here mention your request].*

By the singular merits of thy childhood,
Obtain for us our request.
By thy perfect union with the Divine Will,
Obtain for us our request.
By thy heroic sufferings during thy married life,
[repeat Obtain for us our request after each line]

By the consolation thou didst experience at the conversion
of thy husband,
By the sacrifice of thy children rather than see them
grievously offend God,
By the miraculous entrance into the convent,
By thy severe penances and thrice-daily bloody scourgings,
By the suffering caused by the wound thou didst receive from
the thorn of thy crucified Savior,
By the divine love which consumed thy heart,
By that remarkable devotion to the Blessed Sacrament,
on which alone thou didst exist for four years,
By the happiness with which thou didst part from thy trials
to join thy Divine Spouse,
By the perfect example thou gavest to people of every state
of life.
Pray for us, O holy St. Rita, that we may be made worthy
of the promises of Christ.

LET US PRAY.

O God, who in thine infinite tenderness hast vouchsafed to regard the prayer of thy servant, blessed Rita, and dost grant to her supplication that which is impossible to human foresight, skill, and efforts, in reward of her compassionate love and firm reliance on thy promise, have pity on our adversity and succor us in our calamities, that the unbeliever may know thou art the recompense of the humble, the defense of the helpless, and the strength of those who trust in thee, through Jesus Christ, our Lord. Amen.

Prayer of Jacob Astley for Increased Awareness in All Aspects of Life

Help me today to realize that you will be speaking to me through the events of the day, through people, through things, and through creation. Give me ears, eyes, and heart to perceive you, however veiled your presence may be. Give me insight to see through the exterior of things to the interior truth. Give me your Spirit of discernment. O Lord, you know how busy I must be this day. If I forget you, do not forget me.

Prayer of St. Alphonsus Liguori for Those Suffering from Insomnia

Jesus Christ my God, I adore you and thank you for all the graces you have given me this day. I offer you my sleep and all the moments of this night, and I ask you to keep me from sin. I put myself within your sacred side and under the mantle of Our Lady. Let your holy angels stand about me and keep me in peace. And let your blessing be upon me. Amen.

Prayers for the Gifts of the Holy Spirit

O Spirit of Wisdom, preside over all my thoughts, words, and actions, from this hour until the moment of my death. Spirit of Understanding, enlighten and teach me. Spirit of Counsel, direct my inexperience. Spirit of Fortitude, strengthen my weakness. Spirit of Knowledge, instruct my ignorance. Spirit of Piety, make me fervent in good works. Heavenly Spirit, make me persevere in the service of God, and enable me to act on all occasions with goodness and kindness, charity and joy, with long-suffering, mildness, and fidelity. Let the heavenly virtues of modesty, continency, and chastity adorn the temple you have chosen for your abode. Spirit of Holiness, by your all-powerful grace, preserve me from the misfortune of sin. Amen.

Prayer of Charles Eugène de Foucauld for
When You're at the End of Your Rope

Father, I abandon myself into your hands; do with me what you will. Whatever you may do. I thank you; I am ready for all; I accept all. Let only your will be done in me, and in all your creatures. I wish no more than this, Lord.

Into your hands I commend my soul; I offer it to you with all the love of my heart, for I love you, Lord, and so need to give myself, to surrender myself into your hands, without reserve, and with boundless confidence, for you are my Father.

Prayer to St. John Bosco for Any Need Including Dealing with
Addiction, Assistance for a Sick Parent, Direction for a
Troubled Child, or When You're Struggling at Work

In need of special help, I appeal with confidence to you, O St. John Bosco, for I require not only spiritual graces but also temporal ones, and particularly *[the grace you seek]*. May you, who on earth had such great devotion to Jesus in the Blessed Sacrament, and to Mary, Help of Christians, and who always had compassion for those who were in suffering, obtain from Jesus and from his heavenly Mother the grace I now request, and also a sincere resignation to the will of God.

Prayer of Thomas Merton, "I Have No Idea
Where I Am Going"

(Merton isn't a saint, but his writings are held in high regard by millions of people around the world. This particular passage,

from his book Thoughts in Solitude, *is a favorite of Father James Martin, SJ.)*

My Lord God, I have no idea where I am going. I do not see the road ahead of me. I cannot know for certain where it will end. Nor do I really know myself, and the fact that I think that I am following your will does not mean that I am actually doing so. But I believe that the desire to please you does in fact please you. And I hope I have that desire in all that I am doing. I hope that I will never do anything apart from that desire. And I know that if I do this you will lead me by the right road, though I may know nothing about it. Therefore will I trust you always, though I may seem to be lost and in the shadow of death. I will not fear, for you are ever with me, and you will never leave me to face my perils alone.

Prayer of St. Gemma Galgani During Difficult Times

(St. Gemma Galgani was an Italian nun and mystic whose prayers to the Sacred Heart of Jesus seemingly cured her spinal meningitis. Though this is not a formal prayer, St. Gemma's use of the imagination in her writings radiates with deep love for God. She is known as the patron saint of headaches and migraines, but you can use this prayer whenever you are experiencing hardship and difficulties.)

Imagine that you see a light of immense splendor that penetrates everything and at the same time gives life and animation to all, so that whatever exists has its being from this light and in it lives. Thus I see my God and creatures in him. Imagine a fiery furnace, great as the universe, nay, infinitely greater, that burns everything without consuming anything, and burning illuminates and strengthens, and those who are most penetrated by its flames are happiest, and desire more ardently to be consumed. Thus I see our souls in God.

Novena Prayer to the Infant Jesus of Prague for a Special Intention (Including Troubles with Finances, Relationships, and Health Issues)

One of my favorite devotions, the Infant Jesus of Prague refers to a wooden statue of the Christ child that tradition holds belonged to St. Teresa of Ávila. Sculptures depicting the young Jesus grew in popularity in the Middle Ages and were often put on display during Christmas. The most well-known of these works of art is the one that has been housed in the Church of Our Lady Victorious in Prague since 1628. Though the capital city in Central Europe has been plundered and invaded and has experienced long periods of civil unrest, the statue and the church have remained mostly unscathed for almost four hundred years.

For years, this image of Jesus had been off-putting to me; the ornate, royal garments of the statue seemed the antithesis of the baby born in the manger and wrapped in swaddling clothes that I knew so well from Christmas memories. But I've come to see what millions of others see when they look upon this representation: the richness and miracle of childhood mixed with the kingship of Jesus. It is a reminder of the importance of beholding the hope associated with children. It was a child who changed the world, after all. Tradition holds that the person who can carry a childlike vulnerability in his or her heart—who can be wholly dependent on God the Father—will be blessed in many ways. And while the image of the Infant Jesus of Prague is a reminder of the holiness of childhood, it is also a mirror that reflects back to us the hope we brought into the world when we were born.

The novena associated with this image is one of the most beautiful I've ever prayed. We can meditate on the prayer and the visage of the Christ child whenever we are struggling in life. This devotion is also an exercise in ego deflation. How many adults feel comfortable asking a child for help? We, as adults, are generally the caregivers, the protectors of the innocent. And still, that's what this devotion asks us to do: not worship a statue, but imagine ourselves bowing to a child like those shepherds and wise men did two thousand years ago. Anyone who has sat on the floor and played a game with a child has experienced glimpses of holiness we would never have encountered if we had remained on our feet. So, while it's not necessary, I find praying this prayer on my knees helps me to keep my life, my struggles, and my intentions in perspective.

To be prayed once a day for nine days:

O dearest Jesus, tenderly loving us, your greatest joy is to dwell among us and to bestow your blessing upon us! Though I am not worthy that you should behold me with love, I feel myself drawn to you, O dear infant Jesus, because you gladly pardon me and exercise your almighty power over me.

So many who turned with confidence to you have received graces and had their petitions granted. Behold me, in spirit I kneel before your miraculous image on your altar in Prague, and lay open my heart to you, with its prayers, petitions, and hopes. Especially the affair of *[your request]* I enclose in your loving heart. Govern me and do with me and mine according to your holy will, for I know that in your divine wisdom and love you will ordain everything for the best. Almighty gracious infant Jesus, do not withdraw your hand from us, but protect and bless us forever.

I pray you, sweetest infant, in the name of your Blessed Mother Mary, who cared for you with such tenderness, and by the great reverence with which St. Joseph carried you in his arms, comfort me and make me happy that I may bless and thank you forever from all my heart. Amen.

Prayer of St. John Vianney

(St. John Vianney, also known as the Curé d'Ars, *composed this prayer in the nineteenth century for parish priests, but it should be a prayer that all of us learn by heart today.)*

I love you, O my God, and my only desire is to love you until the last breath of my life. I love you, O infinitely lovable God, and I would rather die loving you, than live without loving you. I love you, Lord, and the only grace I ask is to love you eternally. My God, if my tongue cannot say in every moment that I love you, I want my heart to repeat it to you as often as I draw breath.

APPENDIX II

Calendar of Saints

While the United States has eleven national holidays (not including Super Bowl Sunday), every day is a holiday in the Catholic Church. Each day of the year celebrates the lives of a number of saints. What follows here is a combination of both new and traditional feast days and celebrations that center on Jesus, the Holy Spirit, the saints, the angels, and the Virgin Mary. You can use this calendar as an introduction to the vast number of special souls who have lived and currently live with us in the communion of saints.

JANUARY SAINTS

January 1
> Solemnity of the Blessed Virgin Mary, Mother of God
> Circumcision of Our Lord
> Octave Day of the Nativity

January 2
> St. Basil the Great
> St. Gregory Nazianzen

January 3
Most Holy Name of Jesus
St. Genevieve

January 4
St. Elizabeth Ann Seton

January 5
St. John N. Neumann

January 6
The Epiphany of Our Lord
Sts. Caspar, Balthasar, and Melchior, the three wise men

January 7
St. Lucian of Antioch
St. Raymond of Peñafort

January 8
St. Apollinaris the Apologist
St. Severinus of Noricum

January 9
St. Julian the Hospitalarian and his wife, St. Basilissa
St. Adrian of Canterbury

January 10
St. William of Bourges
St. Nicanor
St. John Camillus the Good

January 11

    St. Theodosius the Cenobiarch

    St. Paulinus

    St. Hyginus

January 12

    St. Benedict Biscop

    St. Arcadius

    St. Marguerite Bourgeoys

January 13

    St. Veronica of Milan

    St. Hilary of Poitiers

    Commemoration of the Baptism of Our Lord

January 14

    St. Felix of Nola

    St. Sava

January 15

    St. Paul the Hermit

    St. Ita of Killeedy

January 16

    St. Fursey

January 17

    St. Antony the Abbot

January 18

    Feast of the Chair of St. Peter at Rome

    St. Volusian

January 19
> St. Canute IV
> St. Wulfstan

January 20
> St. Sebastian
> St. Fabian

January 21
> St. Agnes

January 22
> St. Anastasius XIV

January 23
> St. Vincent, deacon and martyr
> St. Marianne Cope
> St. Emerentiana

January 24
> St. Francis de Sales

January 25
> The Conversion of St. Paul

January 26
> Sts. Timothy and Titus
> St. Paula

January 27
> St. Angela Merici

January 28
> St. Thomas Aquinas
> St. Peter Nolasco

January 29
St. Blath

January 30
St. Bathildes
St. Martina of Rome

January 31
St. John Bosco

FEBRUARY SAINTS

February 1
St. Brigid

February 2
The Feast of the Presentation of Our Lord and
Purification of the Blessed Virgin Mary, also known
as Candlemas Day

February 3
St. Blaise

February 4
St. Andrew Corsini

February 5
St. Agatha

February 6
St. Dorothy
St. Paul Miki

February 7
St. Richard of Lucca

February 8
> St. Jerome Emiliani
> St. Josephine Bakhita

February 9
> St. Apollonia
> St. Nicephorus

February 10
> St. Scholastica

February 11
> Our Lady of Lourdes

February 12
> St. Anthony of Saxony

February 13
> St. Catherine of Ricci

February 14
> St. Valentine
> Sts. Cyril and Methodius (brothers)

February 15
> Sts. Faustinus and Jovita (brothers)
> St. Claude de la Colombière

February 16
> St. Onesimus
> St. Juliana of Nicomedia

February 17
> St. Donatus, martyr

February 18
> St. Flavian of Constantinople

February 19
> St. Barbatus

February 20
> Sts. Francisco Marto and Jacinta Marto (seers of Fatima; siblings)
> St. Eucherius
> St. Amata (Amy)

February 21
> St. Peter Damian

February 22
> Chair of Saint Peter at Antioch

February 23
> St. Polycarp

February 24
> St. Adela

February 25
> St. Tarasius
> St. Walburga

February 26
> St. Alexander

February 27
>St. Leander of Seville

February 28
>St. Romanus
>
>St. Hilary

MARCH SAINTS

March 1
>St. David
>
>St. Albinus

March 2
>Blessed Charles the Good

March 3
>St. Katharine Drexel
>
>St. Cunegundes

March 4
>St. Casimir
>
>St. Lucius I

March 5
>St. John Joseph of the Cross

March 6
>St. Colette
>
>St. Fridolin

March 7
>Sts. Felicitas and Perpetua

March 8
> St. John of God

March 9
> St. Frances of Rome
> St. Gregory of Nyssa

March 10
> St. Victor, martyr

March 11
> St. Eulogius of Cordoba

March 12
> St. Theophanes the Chronicler

March 13
> St. Euphrasia of Constantinople
> St. Roderic

March 14
> St. Matilda

March 15
> St. Louise de Marillac

March 16
> St. Julian of Antioch

March 17
> St. Patrick
> St. Joseph of Arimathea

March 18
> St. Cyril of Jerusalem

March 19
> St. Joseph

March 20
> St. Wulfran
> St. Photina

March 21
> St. Edna

March 22
> St. Nicholas Owen

March 23
> St. Turibius of Mogrovejo
> St. Felix, martyr

March 24
> St. Simon of Trent

March 25
> The Annunciation of the Lord
> St. Dismas

March 26
> St. Ludger

March 27
> St. John of Egypt
> St. Rupert of Salzburg
> St. Augusta

March 28
> St. Alexander, martyr

March 29

    St. Eustace of Luxeuil

March 30

    St. John Climacus

    St. Quirinus of Neuss

March 31

    St. Benjamin

APRIL SAINTS

April 1

    St. Hugh of Grenoble

April 2

    St. Francis of Paola

April 3

    St. Richard of Chichester

    St. Irene of Thessalonica

April 4

    St. Isidore of Seville

April 5

    St. Vincent Ferrer

April 6

    St. Celestine I

April 7

    St. John Baptist de La Salle

April 8

St. Julie Billiart

April 9

St. Gaucherius

April 10

St. Fulbert of Chartres

April 11

St. Stanislaus of Cracow

St. Gemma Galgani

April 12

St. Julius

St. Sabbas the Goth

April 13

St. Hermenegild

St. Martin I

April 14

Sts. Tiburtius, Valerian, and Maximus

St. Lambert of Lyon

April 15

St. Paternus

April 16

St. Bernadette Soubirous

April 17

St. Anicetus

St. Stephen Harding

April 18

    St. Apollonius the Apologist

April 19

    St. Alphege

    St. Leo IX

April 20

    St. Agnes of Montepulciano

April 21

    St. Anselm

    St. Conrad

April 22

    Sts. Epipodius and Alexander

April 23

    St. George

    St. Adalbert

April 24

    St. Fidelis of Sigmaringen

April 25

    St. Mark the Evangelist

April 26

    St. Cletus

    St. Alda

April 27

    St. Zita

April 28

    St. Peter Chanel

    St. Louis de Montfort

April 29

    St. Peter of Verona

    St. Hugh the Great

    St. Catherine of Siena

April 30

    St. Pius V

MAY SAINTS

May 1

    St. Peregrine Laziosi

May 2

    St. Athanasius the Great

May 3

    Sts. Philip and James the Lesser, apostles

    St. Alexander

    St. Juvenal of Narni

May 4

    St. Florian

May 5

    St. Jutta

May 6

    St. Evodius

    Blessed Edward Jones and Anthony Middleton

May 7

St. Domitian of Huy

May 8

St. Desideratus

May 9

St. Pachomius

May 10

St. Damian de Veuster
St. John of Ávila
Sts. Gordian and Epimachus
St. Solange

May 11

St. Francis di Girolama

May 12

Sts. Nereus, Achilleus, and Pancras
St. Pancras

May 13

Our Lady of Fatima

May 14

St. Matthias
St. Boniface of Tarsus

May 15

St. Isidore the Farmer
St. Dymphna

May 16
>   St. John Nepomucen
>   St. Ubaldus
>   St. Brendan the Navigator
>   St. Simon Stock

May 17
>   St. Paschal Baylon

May 18
>   St. Venantius
>   St. John I
>   St. Eric IX of Sweden

May 19
>   St. Pudentiana
>   St. Ivo

May 20
>   St. Bernardine of Siena

May 21
>   St. Christopher Magallanes

May 22
>   St. Rita

May 23
>   St. Julia of Corsica
>   St. John Baptist de Rossi

May 24
>   Sts. Donatian and Rogatian (brothers)
>   St. Joanna

May 25
> St. Bede the Venerable
> St. Mary Magdalene de Pazzi (new)
> St. Urban I

May 26
> St. Philip Neri
> St. Eleutherius

May 27
> St. Augustine of Canterbury

May 28
> St. Bernard of Montjoux

May 29
> St. Maximinus of Trier

May 30
> St. Joan of Arc
> St. Ferdinand III

May 31
> The Visitation of the Virgin Mary

JUNE SAINTS

June 1
> St. Justin, martyr

June 2
> Sts. Marcellinus and Peter

June 3

    St. Charles Lwanga and companions

    St. John XXIII

June 4

    St. Francis Caracciolo

June 5

    St. Boniface of Mainz

June 6

    St. Norbert

June 7

    St. Robert of Newminster

June 8

    Sts. Medard and Gildard (brothers)

June 9

    Sts. Primus and Felician

    St. Columba

    St. Ephrem of Syria

June 10

    St. Landericus

June 11

    St. Barnabas

June 12

    Blessed Jolenta of Poland

June 13

    St. Anthony of Padua

June 14
>St. Elgar

June 15
>Sts. Vitus, Crescentia, and Modestus

June 16
>St. John Francis Regis

June 17
>St. Gregory Barbarigo
>St. Harvey (Hervé)
>St. Botolph

June 18
>Venerable Matt Talbot

June 19
>St. Juliana Falconieri
>St. Romuald
>Sts. Gervase and Protase (brothers)

June 20
>St. Silverius

June 21
>St. Aloysius Gonzaga
>St. Terence

June 22
>St. Paulinus of Nola
>St. John Fisher
>St. Thomas More

June 23
> St. Etheldreda (Audrey)

June 24
> St. John the Baptist

June 25
> St. Prosper of Aquitaine
> St. William of Vercelli

June 26
> Sts. John and Paul
> St. Pelagius
> St. Anthelm

June 27
> St. Cyril of Alexandria
> Our Lady of Perpetual Help

June 28
> St. Irenaeus

June 29
> St. Peter
> St. Paul

June 30
> First Martyrs of the Holy Roman Church

JULY SAINTS

July 1

St. Junípero Serra

July 2

Sts. Processus and Martinian

St. Bernardino Realino

July 3

St. Thomas the Apostle

July 4

St. Theodore of Cyrene

July 5

St. Elizabeth of Portugal

St. Anthony Mary Zaccaria

July 6

St. Maria Goretti

St. Goar

July 7

St. Astius

July 8

St. Grimbald

St. Kilian

July 9

St. Augustine Zhao Rong and companions

July 10

 Sts. Rufina and Secunda (sisters)

July 11

 St. Benedict of Nursia

 St. Pius I

July 12

 St. John Gualbert

 Sts. Nabor and Felix

July 13

 St. Henry II (new)

July 14

 St. Kateri Tekakwitha

July 15

 St. Bonaventure

July 16

 Our Lady of Mount Carmel

July 17

 St. Alexius

July 18

 St. Camillus de Lellis

 St. Frederick

July 19

 St. Arsenius the Great

July 20

    St. Margaret of Antioch

July 21

    St. Lawrence of Brindisi

    St. Praxedes

July 22

    St. Mary Magdalene

July 23

    St. Apollinaris of Ravenna

    St. Bridget of Sweden

    St. Liborius

July 24

    St. Sharbel Makhluf

July 25

    St. James the Greater

    St. Christopher

July 26

    Sts. Joachim and Anne

July 27

    St. Pantaleon

    Sts. Nathalia, Aurelius, Liliosa, Felix, and George

July 28

    Sts. Nazarius and Celsus

July 29

    St. Martha

July 30

    St. Peter Chrysologus

    Sts. Abdon and Sennen

July 31

    St. Ignatius of Loyola

AUGUST SAINTS

August 1

    St. Peter in Chains

    St. Alphonsus Liguori

    Sts. Faith, Hope, and Charity

August 2

    St. Eusebius of Vercelli

    St. Peter Julian Eymard

August 3

    St. Lydia Purpuraria

August 4

    St. John Vianney

August 5

    St. Emygdius

August 6

    The Transfiguration of Our Lord

August 7

    St. Cajetan

August 8

St. Dominic

August 9

St. Teresa Benedicta of the Cross

August 10

St. Lawrence

August 11

Sts. Tiburtius and Susanna

St. Clare of Assisi

St. Philomena

August 12

St. Jane Frances de Chantal

St. Euplius

August 13

St. Radegund

Sts. Pontian and Hippolytus

August 14

St. Maximilian Kolbe

August 15

Assumption of the Blessed Virgin Mary

St. Tarcisius

August 16

St. Roch

August 17
> St. Jeanne Delanoue

August 18
> St. Helena
> St. Agapitus

August 19
> St. John Eudes

August 20
> St. Bernard of Clairvaux

August 21
> St. Pius X

August 22
> The Queenship of the Blessed Virgin Mary

August 23
> St. Philip Benizi
> St. Rose of Lima

August 24
> St. Bartholomew

August 25
> St. Louis IX
> St. Patricia

August 26
> St. Zephyrinus
> Our Lady of Czestochowa

August 27
> St. Monica
> St. Caesarius of Arles

August 28
> St. Augustine of Hippo
> St. Hermes

August 29
> Martyrdom of St. John the Baptist

August 30
> Sts. Felix and Adauctus

August 31
> St. Raymond Nonnatus
> St. Aristides

SEPTEMBER SAINTS

September 1
> St. Giles
> St. Anna the Prophetess

September 2
> St. Agricolus
> St. Ingrid

September 3
> St. Gregory the Great

September 4
> St. Rosalia
> St. Marinus

September 5
>St. Teresa of Calutta
>St. Lawrence Justinian
>St. Bertin

September 6
>St. Eleutherius

September 7
>St. Cloud
>St. Regina

September 8
>St. Adrian
>St. Corbinian

September 9
>St. Peter Claver

September 10
>St. Peter Martinez

September 11
>St. Paphnutius
>St. Adelphus
>Sts. Protus and Hyacinth

September 12
>The Most Holy Name of Mary

September 13
>St. John Chrysostom

September 14

> The Exaltation of the Holy Cross of Our Lord Jesus
> Christ
> St. Maternus
> St. Notburga

September 15

> St. Nicomedes
> Our Lady of Sorrows

September 16

> St. Cyprian
> St. Cornelius
> Sts. Euphemia, Lucy, and Geminianus

September 17

> St. Robert Bellarmine
> St. Hildegard of Bingen
> Feast of the Stigmata of St. Francis of Assisi

September 18

> St. Joseph of Cupertino

September 19

> St. Januarius

September 20

> Sts. Eustachius and companions
> Sts. Andrew Kim Tae-gon, Paul Chong Ha-sang, and
> companions

September 21

> St. Matthew the Apostle

September 22
> St. Thomas of Villanova
> Sts. Maurice and companions

September 23
> St. Thecla
> St. Pius of Pietrelcina (Padre Pio)
> St. Linus
> St. Constantius the Sacristan

September 24
> St. Gerard Sagredo

September 25
> St. Cleophas

September 26
> Blessed Paul VI
> Sts. Cosmas and Damian

September 27
> St. Vincent de Paul

September 28
> St. Wenceslas
> St. Lorenzo Ruiz and companions
> Blessed John of Dukla

September 29
> Sts. Michael, Gabriel, and Raphael, archangels

September 30
> St. Jerome

OCTOBER SAINTS

October 1
St. Thérèse of Lisieux
St. Remigius

October 2
The Holy Guardian Angels

October 3
St. Gerard of Brogne

October 4
St. Francis of Assisi

October 5
St. Faustina Kowalska
Blessed Raymond of Capua
St. Flora of Beaulieu

October 6
St. Bruno
Blessed Marie Rose Durocher

October 7
Our Lady of the Rosary

October 8
St. Pelagia

October 9
> St. Louis Bertrand
> St. John Leonardi
> St. Dionysius the Areopagite

October 10
> St. Francis Borgia

October 11
> St. Firminus

October 12
> St. Wilfrid

October 13
> St. Edward the Confessor
> St. Gerald of Aurillac

October 14
> St. Callistus I

October 15
> St. Teresa of Ávila

October 16
> St. Hedwig
> St. Margaret Mary Alacoque
> St. Gerard Majella

October 17
> St. Ignatius of Antioch

October 18
> St. Luke the Evangelist

October 19
> Sts. John de Brebeuf, Isaac Jogues, and companions

October 20
> St. Paul of the Cross
> St. Irene of Tomar
> Blessed Adeline

October 21
> St. Ursula
> St. Hilarion
> St. Cilinia

October 22
> Pope St. John Paul II
> St. Mary Salome

October 23
> St. John of Capistrano

October 24
> St. Anthony Mary Claret

October 25
> Sts. Crispin and Crispinian
> Sts. Chrysanthus and Daria

October 26
> St. Evaristus
> St. Demetrius

October 27

St. Frumentius

October 28

Sts. Simon and Jude

October 29

St. Narcissus

October 30

St. Alphonsus Rodriguez

October 31

St. Quintin
St. Wolfgang

NOVEMBER SAINTS

November 1

All Saints' Day

November 2

All Souls' Day

November 3

St. Malachy
St. Martin de Porres

November 4

St. Charles Borromeo
Sts. Vitalis and Agricola

November 5
> St. Bertille
> Sts. Zachary and Elizabeth

November 6
> St. Leonard

November 7
> St. Willibrord
> St. Engelbert

November 8
> Four Crowned Martyrs: Severus, Severian, Carpophorus, and Victorinus

November 9
> St. Theodore Tyro

November 10
> St. Andrew Avellino
> St. Leo the Great
> Sts. Tryphon, Respicius, and Nympha

November 11
> St. Martin of Tours
> St. Mennas

November 12
> St. Josaphat

November 13
> St. Frances Xavier Cabrini
> St. Didacus

November 14
> St. Lawrence O'Toole

November 15
> St. Albert the Great
> St. Leopold

November 16
> St. Margaret of Scotland
> St. Gertrude the Great

November 17
> St. Gregory Thaumaturgus

November 18
> St. Rose Philippine Duchesne

November 19
> St. Crispin

November 20
> St. Felix of Valois
> St. Bernward

November 21
> The Presentation of the Blessed Virgin Mary

November 22
> St. Cecilia

November 23
> Pope St. Clement I
> St. Columban
> Blessed Miguel Agustin Pro
> St. Felicitas

November 24
> St. Chrysogonus
> St. Andrew Dung-Lac and companions

November 25
> St. Catherine of Alexandria

November 26
> St. Leonard of Port Maurice
> St. John Berchmans

November 27
> St. Maximus of Reiz
> Our Lady of the Miraculous Medal

November 28
> St. Catherine Labouré

November 29
> St. Saturninus (see November 28)

November 30
> St. Andrew
> St. Maura

DECEMBER SAINTS

December 1
    St. Eligius
    St. Edmund Campion

December 2
    St. Bibiana

December 3
    St. Frances Xavier

December 4
    St. John Damascene

December 5
    St. Sabas
    St. Gerald

December 6
    St. Nicholas

December 7
    St. Ambrose

December 8
    Feast of the Immaculate Conception of the Blessed
        Virgin Mary

December 9
    St. Leocadia
    St. Juan Diego

December 10
Pope St. Gregory III

December 11
St. Damasus

December 12
Our Lady of Guadalupe

December 13
St. Lucy

December 14
St. John of the Cross
St. Venantius Fortunatus

December 15
St. Mary Di Rosa

December 16
St. Adelaide

December 17
St. Olympias

December 18
St. Gatian

December 19
Blessed Urban V

December 20
St. Dominic of Silos

December 21
> St. Peter Canisius

December 22
> Sts. Chaeremon and Ischyrion

December 23
> St. Servulus

December 24
> Sts. Adam and Eve
> Vigil of Christmas

December 25
> The Nativity of Christ
> St. Anastasia III

December 26
> St. Stephen the first martyr

December 27
> St. John the evangelist

December 28
> The Holy Innocents

December 29
> St. Thomas Becket of Canterbury

December 30
> St. Sabinus

December 31
> St. Sylvester I

PERMISSIONS

Every reasonable effort has been made to determine copyright holders of excerpted materials and to secure permissions as needed. If any copyright materials have been inadvertently used in this work without proper credit being given in one form or another, please notify Penguin Random House in writing so that future printings of this work may be corrected accordingly.

Scripture quotations are from New Revised Standard Version Bible, © 1989 by National Council of the Churches of Christ in the United States of America. Used by permission. All rights reserved worldwide.

The image of Divine Mercy and the Divine Mercy Novena used with permission of the Marian Fathers of the Immaculate Conception of the BVM.

Prayer to St. Gerard, © Frank Pavone. Used with permission of Priests for Life.

Prayer to St. Jude, © St. Jude League/National Shrine of St. Jude. Used with permission. www.shrineofstjude.org.

Prayer to St. Peregrine from *Catholic Prayers for All Occasions*, © 2017 by Jacquelyn Lindsey. Used with permission of Our Sunday Visitor.

Novena and prayers of the Miraculous Medal used with permission of Father Kevin McCracken, C.M., Association of the Miraculous Medal.

ACKNOWLEDGMENTS

I must lead here by thanking my dear friend Maura Poston Zagrans. Maura was my backup reader on this project, and all along the way she challenged my words and ideas in positive and affirming ways. Thank you, Maura, for your insight, creativity, and most important, your friendship.

I am deeply indebted to Kathryn Lopez for her support and daily prayers during the writing of this book. Kathryn and I have grown in friendship and mutual admiration for each other over the years and I value her insight, good humor, and spiritual passion.

Many thanks go to Mitch Horowitz, my editor at Penguin Random House, for his support and feedback. And thank you to the team at TarcherPerigee including Julia Chang, Heather Brennan, Jillian Fata, Sabila Khan, Lorna Henry, and Kym Surridge.

Special thanks to Crista Maracic for her friendship, curiosity, enthusiasm, and intelligence and for inspiring new ideas in me; Father Michael Holleran for his ebullient support and keen editorial eye; Ann Ball, whose excellent book *Encyclopedia of Catholic Devotions and Practices* helped fill in the gaps of my own knowledge; Thomas J. Craughwell for his assistance on the angels chapter; and all the good folks at Loyola Press who have supported my work over the years including Tom McGrath, Joe Durepos, Joellyn Cicciarelli, Santiago Cortés-Sjöberg, Maria Cuadrado, Vinita

Wright, Yvonne Micheletti, Sophie Lorenzo, Rosemary Lane, Becca Russo, Denise Gorss, Judine O'Shea, and Andrew Yankech.

Thank you to the following for their dedication, support, and friendship: Eric Hafker, Michael Stephenson, Will "Sticks" Romano, Kimberly Snyder, Deepak Chopra, Scott Hahn, Michael Singer, Joan Chittister, James Martin, George Weigel, Brant Pitre, Brandon Vogt, Bishop Andrzej Zglejszewski, Bishop Robert Barron, James Hansen, Joseph Scolaro, Anna Keating, Christine Namen, Steve Cobb, Carie Freimuth, Jennifer Stallone Riddell, and Victoria Skurnick.

Thank you to Frances, Josephine, Lenny, and Carrie Poppi for all your love, patience, direction, and kindness over the years. I couldn't be luckier to call you family.

Thank you to my mom for all your love and in supporting me on this project. You are the most courageous person I know and I'm proud to be your son. And thank you to my sisters, Annie, Mary, Suzie, and Julie, for your love and support.

Thanks to my dad, wherever you may be.

As always, thank you to the loves of my life, Grace, Eddie, and Charlie. I am honored, blessed, and so happy to be in your lives.

Heavenly Father, pray for us.

ABOUT THE AUTHOR

Gary Jansen is the director of Image Books and a senior editor at Penguin Random House, where he has edited and published books by *New York Times* bestselling authors Pope Benedict XVI, Pope Francis, Michael Singer, Deepak Chopra, and Kimberly Snyder. He is the author of the critically acclaimed memoir *Holy Ghosts: Or, How a (Not So) Good Catholic Boy Became a Believer in Things That Go Bump in the Night; The 15-Minute Prayer Solution;* and *Station to Station*. Paulo Coelho, *New York Times* bestselling author of *The Alchemist*, has called Jansen's work "wonderful," while legendary *Newsweek* religion editor Kenneth L. Woodward has called him "a fine writer." A frequent lecturer, Jansen has appeared on NPR, CNN.com, Coast to Coast AM, SundanceTV, the Travel Channel, and A&E. His writing has been featured in the *Huffington Post, Religion Dispatches*, and *USA Today*. He lives in New York with his wife and two sons. Visit him at www.garyjansen.com.